This important collection re-examines origins and tra_____ scholarly field of educational inquiry. Maria Manzon_____ group of specialists whose papers challenge many exi_____ ment. Volker Lenhart, for example, draws attention t_____ Antoine Jullien, Christel Adick reminds us of the worl_____ association with Bereday's four-step model of comparison, and Erw_____ writes of the *International Education Review*'s ideological usurpation under Nazism. Robert Cowen contributes a lively paper on key actors and 'ways of knowing', Felicitas Acosta and Guillermo Ramón Ruiz describe ways in which comparative education has developed in Latin America, and Keita Takayama articulates the 'area studies' tradition in comparative inquiry, with particular reference to Japan. Together, their papers provide a fresh look at comparative education and its history that will be of interest to all concerned with understanding what this important dimension of educational inquiry is about.

–David Phillips, *Emeritus Professor of Comparative Education, University of Oxford, UK*

Origins and Traditions in Comparative Education

This volume aims to expand knowledge about the history of comparative education. It explores new scholarship on key actors and ways of knowing in the field. It aims to raise awareness on the positionality of historical narratives about this field of inquiry and offers a re-think of its histories.

Since comparative education has always been embedded within a global field of power, what would the changing world order's implications be for the institutional and intellectual histories of the field? This book offers diverse perspectives for re-theorising the histories of comparative education. It suggests casting a far-sighted and panoramic look at the field's origins. The volume concludes with a puzzle for future work on a global history of comparative education.

This book was originally published as a special issue of *Comparative Education*.

Maria Manzon is Assistant Professor at the Education University of Hong Kong. She is an Associate Editor of the *Asia Pacific Education Journal*. She is also a Board Member of the Comparative Education Society of Asia and was previously Chair of the Admissions and New Societies Standing Committee of the World Council of Comparative Education Societies.

Origins and Traditions in Comparative Education

Edited by
Maria Manzon

Routledge
Taylor & Francis Group

LONDON AND NEW YORK

First published 2019
by Routledge
2 Park Square, Milton Park, Abingdon, Oxon, OX14 4RN

and by Routledge
605 Third Avenue, New York, NY 10017

First issued in paperback 2020

Routledge is an imprint of the Taylor & Francis Group, an informa business

© 2019 Taylor & Francis

British Library Cataloguing in Publication Data
A catalogue record for this book is available from the British Library

ISBN 13: 978-0-367-72829-8 (pbk)
ISBN 13: 978-0-367-25361-5 (hbk)

Typeset in Myriad Pro
by RefineCatch Limited, Bungay, Suffolk

Publisher's Note
The publisher accepts responsibility for any inconsistencies that may have arisen during the conversion of this book from journal articles to book chapters, namely the inclusion of journal terminology.

Disclaimer
Every effort has been made to contact copyright holders for their permission to reprint material in this book. The publishers would be grateful to hear from any copyright holder who is not here acknowledged and will undertake to rectify any errors or omissions in future editions of this book.

Contents

Citation Information

The chapters in this book were originally published in *Comparative Education*, volume 54, issue 1 (February 2018). When citing this material, please use the original page numbering for each article, as follows:

Chapter 6
Towards a new articulation of comparative educations: cross-culturalising research imaginations
Keita Takayama
Comparative Education, volume 54, issue 1 (February 2018), pp. 77–93

Chapter 7
Comparative education histories: a postscript
Maria Manzon
Comparative Education, volume 54, issue 1 (February 2018), pp. 94–107

For any permission-related enquiries please visit:
http://www.tandfonline.com/page/help/permissions

Notes on Contributors

Felicitas Acosta is a Researcher and Professor at the Universidad Nacional de General Sarmiento, Argentina. She teaches History of Education, Comparative Education, and Educational Foundations. She is Vice President of the Argentine Society of Comparative Studies in Education and founding member and past editor of *Revista Latinoamericana de Educación Comparada*.

Christel Adick is Emeritus Professor of Comparative Education, in which she held the Chair from 1993–2013, at the Ruhr-Universität Bochum, Germany. She was a member of the editorial board of the *International Review of Education* (2000–2010), under the auspices of the UNESCO Institute Hamburg, and continues to be active in various national and international academic associations.

Robert Cowen is an Honorary Member of the Comparative Education Society in Europe and Professor Emeritus at the University College London Institute of Education, UK (formerly the Institute of Education, University of London, to which he was appointed in 1976). His current main interest is the theoretical condition of comparative education.

Erwin H. Epstein is Professor Emeritus of Cultural and Educational Policy Studies at Loyola University Chicago, USA. He is a former President of both the Comparative and International Education Society and the World Council of Comparative Education Societies. He was the editor for 10 years of the *Comparative Education Review*.

Volker Lenhart is Professor Emeritus at the Institute of Education at Heidelberg University, Germany. He publishes in the fields of foundation of education, history of education, and school as a social institution. In comparative and international education, he is active in research and consultancy for educational development cooperation, and recently in human rights and peace education.

Maria Manzon is Assistant Professor at the Education University of Hong Kong. She is an Associate Editor of the *Asia Pacific Education Journal*. She is also a Board Member of the Comparative Education Society of Asia and was previously Chair of the Admissions and New Societies Standing Committee of the World Council of Comparative Education Societies.

Guillermo Ramón Ruiz is Senior Professor of Theories of Education and Educational Policy at the Universidad de Buenos Aires, Argentina, and a Researcher at the National Scientific and Technical Research Council of Argentina (CONICET). His work examines educational reforms. He is co-editor of the journal *Foro de Educación*.

Keita Takayama is a Professor at the Graduate School of Education, Kyoto University, Japan and Director for its Global Education Office. Many of his writings have appeared in *Comparative Education* and *Comparative Education Review*.

Origins and traditions in comparative education: challenging some assumptions

Maria Manzon ⓘ

ABSTRACT
This article questions some of our assumptions about the history of comparative education. It explores new scholarship on key actors and ways of knowing in the field. Building on the theory of the social constructedness of the field of comparative education, the paper elucidates how power shapes our scholarly histories and identities.

Introduction

The year 2017 commemorated several significant moments in the intellectual histories of comparative education, which could be categorised into three 'epistemological benchmarks': positivism, relativism, and historical functionalism (Epstein 2008, 373). First, it marked the bicentenary of Marc-Antoine Jullien de Paris' 1817 publication of *Esquisse et vues préliminaires d'un ouvrage sur l'éducation comparée* [Plan and Preliminary Views of a Work on Comparative Education]. Jullien's text tends to be regarded as the beginning of comparative education as a positivist field of study (Hans 1962; Bereday 1964; Noah and Eckstein 1969; Epstein 2008). Second, 2017 was also the 160th anniversary of K. D. Ushinsky's (1857) work *On National Character of Public Education*, which ushered in a second epistemological platform for comparative education: relativism. Lastly, it marked the 70th anniversary of Friedrich Schneider's (1947) opus, *Triebkräfte der Pädagogik der Völker*, which identifies with another epistemological platform of comparative education, namely historical functionalism. It is worth mentioning that 2017 also marked the centennial of the first Chinese volume entitled *Comparative Study of National Education in Germany, France, Britain and the USA* (Yu 1917). These anniversaries are timely signposts for stocktaking. What do these different landmarks mean for us today and for our future? How did they acquire the status of becoming landmarks in the first place and for what end?

Historical narratives of academic disciplines have different purposes. They introduce newcomers into a field. They legitimate a field's intellectual territory to external parties. They also serve as political gatekeepers of a field, justifying change or preventing it (Klein 1993). Some origin stories aim to establish the image of a field as a true science. The histories of comparative education perform similar functions.

Interpreting the past depends on the lenses used to read it. You see as far and as clearly as your lenses permit you. A modernist view would see the past in terms of unity, continuity, cumulative progress as in a linear, unidirectional, and teleological fashion. By contrast, postmodernist stances perceive discontinuity, reversal, contingency, and conflict. This perspective is reinforced by Foucault's concept of 'genealogies' (1980) referring to his critique of the power-knowledge relations constituting fields of knowledge. Thus, 'genealogies' is used here not in its conventional meaning of a linear chronology or family tree of scholars and institutions (e.g. Wilson 1994), but as a 'counter-history of ideas'. It views disciplinary histories in terms of discontinuity and disjuncture and puts into question meta-narratives of the 'official' historical stages of development that disciplines usually offer as a history of ideas.

This article casts a critical eye on comparative education historiography. Its point of departure is that comparative education – the field as its histories – is socially constructed. Its aim is to raise awareness on the positionality of the historical narratives about our field. It offers an analytical framework to position our histories of comparative education, both old and new.

Constructed histories

As I argued extensively elsewhere, comparative education is a constructed field (Manzon 2011). It is 'constructed both institutionally and intellectually. Sociological and epistemological forms of power interact dialectically in shaping the field's contours' (Manzon 2011, 221). The sociological core of a field exhibits particular, contingent, and changing features, while its epistemological component has universal, necessary, and permanent characteristics. Thus, the institutional construction of comparative education as a distinct field, in the form of academic courses and professional societies, depends not on cognitive criteria alone. Rather it is the product of pragmatic and political forces working through a complex interaction of power relations among discourses, social structures and human agency (ibid.). The substantial establishment of comparative education at universities in North America and parts of Western Europe after World War II (1945–70) shows the clear relationship between power and knowledge. Actors who had the appropriate types of capital gained positions of power in the intellectual field. Similarly, but with a reverse effect, academic comparative education was de-legitimised in the universities of the Eastern bloc, and comparativists 're-educated'. Geopolitical power thus influenced what counted as useful knowledge. This is the institutional construction of comparative education.

In parallel, comparative education is also constructed intellectually. Its academic definitions are shaped not by purely intellectual criteria. Rather, they are the outcome of contestations among academics – with their habitus, micro-political interests, forms of capital and disinterested scholarship – to define the field. Moreover, scholars form discursive constellations which occupy unequal positions of power in the global economy of knowledge production. Some, due to their paradigmatic position in the geopolitical world, likewise occupy a central position in the knowledge field. Their epistemology enjoys hegemony and serves as a model for those in the periphery. Thus, definitions of comparative education are positional (Manzon 2011, 212; see also Anweiler 1977; Kelly, Altbach, and Arnove 1982; Cowen 1990; Marginson and Mollis 2002). Academics compete for intellectual territory and the legitimacy of their definitions, methodologies and purposes of comparative education.

The interplay between the sociological and the epistemological and its impact on the intellectual and institutional construction of comparative education is shown in Figure 1. The analytical framework helps to map the diverse intellectual and institutional histories of comparative education. The interaction between sociological and epistemological power become translated into intellectual discourses (e.g. academic definitions, purposes, methods) and institutional structures (e.g. courses, publications, professional societies). Furthermore, comparative education can be plotted as a continuum of specialisation (distinct identity) and broadening or integration (no distinct identity).

More importantly, agency by the comparativist is crucial in this framework. As I claimed, definitions of comparative education are

> based not only on certain epistemological structures, but also on cumulative work done in the field … and on the position of power and breadth of vision of the academic defining the field in relation to other positions in the field. (Manzon 2011, 212)

Why another histories?

Because we suffer from historical amnesia and myopia. This is despite the existence of significant work by eminent scholars on the histories of comparative education gathered in the two volumes of the *International Handbook of Comparative Education* (Cowen and Kazamias 2009), with several chapters contributed by Andreas Kazamias himself, a trained historian (Kazamias 2009a, 2009b). In general, the historical dimension is missing in comparative studies of education (Phillips 2014). Also, the lack of a 'sustained sense of the field's historical development' (Cook, Hite, and Epstein 2004, 146) remains a challenge for identity formation in this growing global community (Epstein 2017a). There is too the vincible ignorance of comparativists or those who profess to be so. Paradoxically,

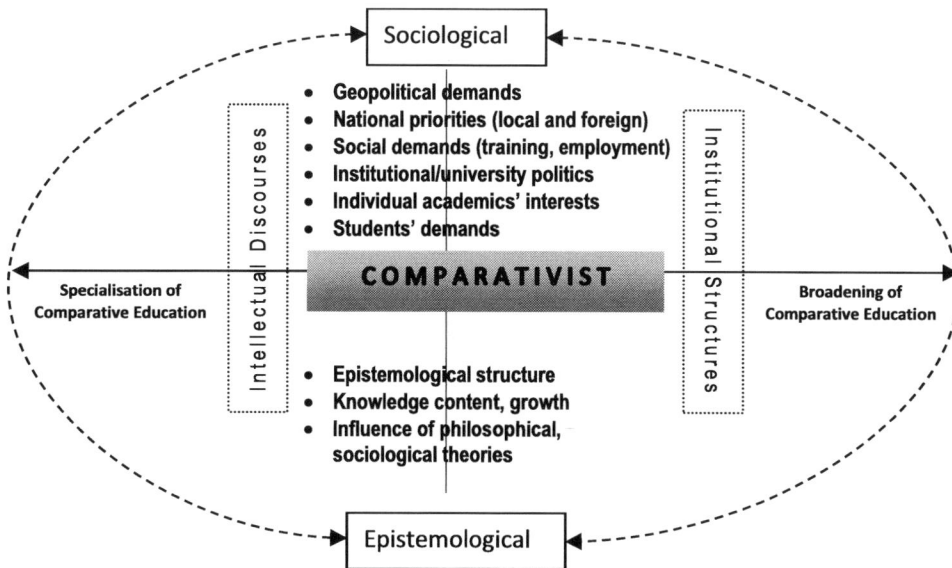

Figure 1. Intellectual and institutional construction of comparative education. Source: Manzon (2011, 222).

we are more *doers* rather than knowers of comparative education. This article seeks to provoke some anamnesis and intellectual curiosity about our unknown pasts. It also hopes to challenge the field's *doxa* on its iconic ancestors. Some of the questions to be explored below echo the challenge posed by Cowen (2009, 8) for a comparative history of comparative education to be written.

- What are the alternative foundational epistemologies of comparative education?
- Who were the major comparative educationists in different eras and locations, and what kinds of people were they? How did their professional life stories construct the diverse histories of comparative education? How can we deconstruct and reconstruct our field's iconographies?
- What alternative genealogies of comparative education might be identified in different parts of the world, by different groups, according to different themes? What are the histories of our institutional programmes in different centres of gravity?
- Why have these alternative discourses remained unknown or forgotten in the English-language literature until now?
- Why are these alternative knowledges important today, or are they important at all and for whom? In what way do they reconstruct the field of comparative education?

By re-constructing our histories from the prism of how power shapes our scholarly endeavours, we comparativists can hopefully reject the temptation of power and re-discover the rightful place of academic comparative education as a critique to the instrumentalisation of knowledge by and for power.

New pasts

The articles in this volume offer new perspectives to these perennial questions. They can also be mapped onto the analytical framework discussed above and shown in Figure 1. Yet they are but a drop in the ocean compared to the unseen histories that still need to be written.

Intellectual histories of the field are insightful and useful. However, they may be reductionist and appear as disembodied histories of ideas. The opening article by Robert Cowen (2017) addresses this lacuna with a new interpretation of the history of comparative education seen through the interactions between comparative scholars' individual biography, professional work space and personal 'readings of the global' in response to macro-political and social environments. He compares four luminaries in the field: Nigel Grant, Joseph Lauwerys, Brian Holmes, and Edmund King. The latter three were his teachers at the Institute of Education, University of London. The article offers a brief but convincing theory on the role of a scholar's 'reading of the global' in re-constructing comparative education. It clearly illustrates the positionality of comparativists' intellectual discourses – their ways of knowing and doing – about comparative education. It shows the sociological-epistemological dialectic in each scholar. Thus, from the hierarchical positions of power that comparativists occupy in the intellectual field, they construct the field of comparative education through scholarly discourses about methods, field definitions and purposes.

Following this thread of embodied comparative education, the second article by Volker Lenhart (2017) proposes Friedrich August Hecht's historical-philosophical-idiographic methodology as an alternative foundational epistemology to Jullien's positivist approach. Lenhart situates Hecht's epistemology in the socio-historical context of the late 18th century, antedating Jullien's work by two decades. Lenhart's article dovetails the insightful research of Epstein (2017b) on other possible founders of comparative education. It also highlights two important lessons. First, comparative education, for Hecht, was not about international policy borrowing and lending, but about interpretation and deep understanding or *Verstehen*. Second, Hecht infused his professional bias as a trained philologist into his comparative education methodology. This ushered in the importance of establishing the truth over pursuing utility in comparative studies.

Of a similar genre of historical research on the field's methodological origins is the work of Christel Adick (2017) on the ancestry of the 'four steps of comparison model' largely attributed to George Z. F. Bereday (1964) in the Anglo-American literature, but to Franz Hilker (1962) in German scholarship. Similar to the previous two articles (Cowen 2017; Lenhart 2017), this article embeds the methodological discourses of Hilker and Bereday in their professional life stories and elucidates the two scholars' fruitful 'symbiotic' relationship. Key to this relationship was the multilingual competency of Hilker and Bereday. The lack of multilingual capital among comparativists limits their intellectual horizon and discourses. It insulates communities of scholars and draws invisible boundaries to scholarship. This probably accounts, to some extent, for the blinkered histories of our field. Yet another form of power constrained comparative education, as exemplified in Hilker's life: political power during the Nazi regime. Hilker was dismissed from his academic post in 1933 and had to re-start his career after World War II. Political power thus de-legitimised comparative education knowledge.

The disruptive potential of geopower under the Nazi era in the 1930s is elaborated in the article of Erwin H. Epstein (2017a). The article breaks the silence on the existence of the *International Education Review* (IER), the first international journal on the field founded in 1930 by Friedrich Schneider of Germany and later joined by American Paul Monroe as co-editor. In 1934, Schneider was dismissed from his academic posts; Nazi ideologue Alfred Baumler replaced him as IER editor. Epstein relates how the IER became an instrument of Nazi ideology, what he denominates as 'a dark episode' in the early institutional history of the field. This episode evokes similar patterns of disruption and de-legitimisation of comparative education institutions and discourses in the then Socialist Bloc in Eastern Europe (1945–1989) as well as in countries where communism (e.g. China from 1949–1976) or nationalism (e.g. South Africa, Chile, and Brazil in the 1960s) prevailed. Comparative education knowledge became 'power-disabled' because its knowledge was perceived to be 'power-disabling' by those who dominated the field of political power (Manzon 2011, 116). National and international politics thus constrained intellectual discourse, in the Foucauldian sense. It limited what could be said and written about in comparative education during the period in the affected countries. This is expected. Epstein (2017a), however, moves scholarship forward by revealing the phenomenon of academic complicity in the Nazi project within the history of comparative education.

Counter-paradigmatic?

Thus far, the new histories that I have surveyed above are located in the paradigmatic centre of comparative education. They are based in Anglo-American and European ambits. Most of them are micro-histories of individual comparativists and how their scholarly work served as the discursive medium through which 'multi-level power relations between structure-agency and epistemology are codified' (Manzon 2011, 224). These discourses take shape in the institutional structures and intellectual definitions of the field. In terms of institutionalisation, 'paradigmatic' academic comparative education is usually located at universities and/or teacher training colleges. They tend to precede the formation of professional societies (Manzon 2011, 76) and take a leading role in knowledge production. As for intellectual discourses, Anglophone scholarship tends to dominate and eclipse indigenous comparative education epistemologies of other linguistic communities. This section introduces two narratives that disturb the paradigm. The first focuses on a world region; the second takes a national comparative education society as the unit of analysis.

A discontinuity in the institutional histories of comparative education is the case of Latin America. In their article, Felicitas Acosta and Guillermo Ruiz (2017) claim that the field in Latin America has a unique 'way of being' which diverges from paradigmatic comparative education. First, institutionalisation is not university-based; national government and international organisations dominate the production and use of comparative education knowledge. The establishment or revival of comparative education societies in the region in the 2000s has given voice and shape to university academics. Second, the purpose of comparative education is to guide educational policy and planning of basic education. This specific 'way of being' of the field emerged against the backdrop of financial crises and structural reforms of educational systems in the region. Macro-economic structure, international political histories, and the relatively eclipsed role of higher education, have distinctively shaped the field in Latin America.

Another discontinuity, albeit to the paradigmatic intellectual history of comparative education, is the research of Keita Takayama (2017) on the epistemological tradition of the Japan Comparative Education Society (JCES). The key contribution of this article is its apologia for a particular intellectual tradition within JCES – area-studies – as a way to provincialise the paradigmatic social scientific approaches in Anglophone comparative education scholarship. Drawing on interviews of 25 JCES members, Takayama gives voice to Japanese scholars contesting theory-driven research by European and North American counterparts. The JCES case reinforces the discussion above about the intellectual construction of comparative education. Its intellectual discourses continue to be reshaped by contestations among scholars – whose habitus, cultural traditions, micro-political interests, forms of capital – define the field. Academics compete for intellectual legitimacy of their definitions, methodologies and purposes of comparative education. Yet such productive contestations are only possible through a transnational language and, above all, a transnational outlook.

Unwritten histories

Maps are like histories. They are never disembodied eyes onto the world they seek to represent. A map is a 'continual negotiation between its makers and users, as their understanding of the world changes' (Brotton 2014, 437). It offers an interpretation of the world based on prevalent assumptions. Likewise, histories interpret the past through the prism of the present and form part of 'eschatological' worldviews. They are con- structed narratives of time past written for specific purposes and addressed to specific audiences.

This volume offers a re-think of the histories of comparative education. It explores both paradigmatic and counter-paradigmatic stories. It exposes a wide uncharted territory for comparative scholars. In the final article of this volume, Manzon (in press) adopts a catho- lic, all-embracing lens to re-theorise comparative education histories. Building on Epstein (2017b) who has asked the question about 'the origins' of comparative education, she suggests that the genesis narratives of paradigmatic comparative education could be more far-sighted. New thinking on the field's histories may benefit from a universal space-time lens that captures new (and yet older) forms of comparisons of educations that had been undertaken in ancient and pre-modern cosmopolitan societies prior to the European colonial era. The article is also forward-looking. Since comparative education histories have always been embedded within a global field of power, what would the changing world order's implications be on the institutional and intellectual histories of the field? The succeeding generations of comparativists may need to keep a close (yet open) eye on history.

Disclosure statement

No potential conflict of interest was reported by the author.

ORCID

Maria Manzon ⓘ http://orcid.org/0000-0003-4946-5688

References

Acosta, F., and G. R. Ruiz. 2017. "Revisiting Comparative Education in Latin America: Traditions, Uses and Perspectives." *Comparative Education*. doi:10.1080/03050068.2017.1400760.
Adick, C. 2017. "Bereday and Hilker: Origins of the 'Four Steps of Comparison' Model." *Comparative Education*. doi:10.1080/03050068.2017.1396088.
Anweiler, O. 1977. "Comparative Education and the Internationalization of Education." *Comparative Education* 13 (2): 109–114.
Bereday, G. Z. F. 1964. *Comparative Method in Education*. New York: Holt, Rinehart and Winston.
Brotton, J. 2014. *A History of the World in 12 Maps*. New York: Penguin Books.

Cook, B. J., S. J. Hite, and E. H. Epstein. 2004. "Discerning Trends, Contours, and Boundaries in Comparative Education: A Survey of Comparativists and Their Literature." *Comparative Education Review* 48 (2): 123–149.

Cowen, R. 1990. "The National and International Impact of Comparative Education Infrastructures." In *Comparative Education: Contemporary Issues and Trends*, edited by W. D. Halls, 321–352. Paris: UNESCO; London: Jessica Kingsley.

Cowen, R. 2009. "On History and On the Creation of Comparative Education." In *International Handbook of Comparative Education*, edited by R. Cowen and A. M. Kazamias, 7–10. Dordrecht: Springer.

Cowen, R. 2017. "Embodied Comparative Education." *Comparative Education*. doi: 10.1080/03050068. 2017.1409554.

Cowen, R., and A. M. Kazamias, eds. 2009. *International Handbook of Comparative Education*. Dordrecht: Springer.

Epstein, E. H. 2008. "Setting the Normative Boundaries: Crucial Epistemological Benchmarks in Comparative Education." *Comparative Education* 44 (4): 373–386.

Epstein, E. H. 2017a. "The Nazi Seizure of the *International Education Review*: A Dark Episode in the Early Professional Development of Comparative Education." *Comparative Education*. doi:10. 1080/03050068.2017.1396092.

Epstein, E. H. 2017b. "Is Marc-Antoine Jullien de Paris the 'Father' of Comparative Education?" *Compare: A Journal of Comparative and International Education* 47 (3): 317–331.

Foucault, M. 1980. *Power/Knowledge: Selected Interviews and Other Writings 1972–1977*. London: Harvester Press.

Hans, N. 1962. "K. D. Ushinsky: Russian Pioneer of Comparative Education." *Comparative Education Review* 5 (3): 162–166.

Hilker, F. 1962. *Vergleichende Pädagogik*. München: Max Hueber.

Jullien, M.-A. 1817. *Esquisse et Vues Préliminaires d'un Ouvrage sur l'Éducation Comparée*. Paris: Société Établie à Paris pour l'Amélioration de l'Enseignement Elémentaire. Reprinted 1962. Genève: Bureau International d'Éducation.

Kazamias, A. M. 2009a. "Forgotten Men, Forgotten Themes: The Historical-Philosophical-Cultural and Liberal Humanist Motif in Comparative Education." In *International Handbook of Comparative Education*, edited by R. Cowen, and A. M. Kazamias, 37–58. Dordrecht: Springer.

Kazamias, A. M. 2009b. "Reclaiming a Lost Legacy: The Historical Humanist Vision in Comparative Education." In *International Handbook of Comparative Education*, edited by R. Cowen, and A. M. Kazamias, 1267–1276. Dordrecht: Springer.

Kelly, G. P., P. Altbach, and R. Arnove. 1982. "Trends in Comparative Education: A Critical Analysis." In *Comparative Education*, edited by P. Altbach, R. Arnove, and G. P. Kelly, 505–533. New York: Collier MacmillanKlein.

Klein, J. T. 1993. "Blurring, Cracking, and Crossing: Permeation and the Fracturing of Discipline." In *Knowledges: Historical and Critical Studies of Disciplinarity*, edited by E. Messer-Davidson, D. R. Sumway, and D. J. Sylvan, 185–211. Charlottesville: University of Virginia.

Lenhart, V. 2017. "Hechtius (1795–1798) – The Beginnings of Historical-Philosophical-Idiographic Research in Comparative Education." *Comparative Education*. doi:10.1080/03050068.2017. 1396094.

Manzon, M. 2011. *Comparative Education: The Construction of a Field*. Hong Kong: Comparative Education Research Centre. The University of Hong Kong, and Dordrecht: Springer.

Manzon, M. in press. "Comparative Education Histories: A Postscript." *Comparative Education*.

Marginson, S., and M. Mollis. 2002. "The Door Opens and the Tiger Leaps: Theories and Reflexivities of Comparative Education for a Global Millennium." *Comparative Education Review* 45 (4): 581–615.

Noah, H. J., and M. A. Eckstein. 1969. *Toward a Science of Comparative Education*. New York: Macmillan.

Phillips, D. 2014. "'Comparatography', History and Policy Quotation: Some Reflections." *Comparative Education* 50 (1): 73–83.

Schneider, F. 1947. *Triebkräfte der Pädagogik der Völker*. Salzburg: Otto Müller Verlag.

Takayama, K. 2017. "Towards a New Articulation of Comparative Educations: Cross-culturalising Research Imaginations." *Comparative Education*. doi:10.1080/03050068.2017.1401303.

Ushinsky, K. D. 1857. "On National Character of Public Education." Reprinted 1975, In *K.D. Ushinsky: Selective Works*, edited by A. J. Piskunov, 100–207. Moscow: Progress.

Wilson, D. N. 1994. "Comparative and International Education: Fraternal or Siamese Twins? A Preliminary Genealogy of Our Twin Fields." *Comparative Education Review* 38 (4): 449–486.

Yu, J. 1917. *Comparative Study of National Education in Germany, France, Britain and the USA.* Shanghai: China Book Co. [in Chinese].

Embodied comparative education

Robert Cowen

ABSTRACT

One way to look at some of the scholars in English-language comparative education in the 1960s is to see them as being concerned with 'methods'. They themselves emphasised that they were re-thinking 'method' in comparative education. Victories were won and courses were rewritten. That 'historic' moment is taught (if it is taught at all nowadays, because history can be made to disappear) as if all that was at stake is mistakes in method. The general argument of this article is that the complex kaleidoscope of our history can and should be tapped. There was more to the scholars of the 1960s than mere 'method', and there is more to be learned from them, for us now. At a time when – especially in England – it is becoming conventional to stress the importance of technically rigorous empirical fieldwork as the kind of 'robust and relevant research' work that politicians and national academic quality control agencies think the nation needs – it is sensible to pause and ask: is our 'history' of the 1960s, with its remarkable emphasis on discussions about method, a simplification of something more complex? What have we been missing? What questions should we take to the archives, to illuminate the present?

Introduction

When I returned from the USA to work in the Institute of Education in the University of London, one of my former teachers Professor Joseph Lauwerys used to invite me, from time to time, to be a house guest for the weekend. Sometimes the weekend of discussions would begin before I had successfully carried the suitcases into the house and debate tended to be intense, at least until dinner time approached. Then attention would shift to equally important things, such as the wines he would serve for dinner. One evening, just as partridges – the main course – were about to be served, Lauwerys suddenly asked his wife: 'Where is the asparagus?' The answer that there was no asparagus produced a dramatic reaction. I was given a torch and Lauwerys took up a spade. We spent some minutes, in the dark, digging up asparagus in the garden before Lauwerys, having trimmed and washed the asparagus spears, asked that they be cooked.

At that moment, I saw in Lauwerys something which I had not fully grasped, despite having a sense of the life histories of colleagues whom I admired. Lauwerys, in some peculiar intangible, almost Sadlerian sense, was an embodiment of 'comparative education' and identities formed long ago. Digging up asparagus by torchlight while good wines and carefully cooked food awaited us seemed to me to be a mysterious, startling glimpse into another cultural world that had different first principles. There was a world-view here, beyond my ken.

As it happens, I also knew personally Brian Holmes and Edmund J. King. Brian Holmes, in his retirement in particular, took up the hobby of fixing classical timepieces – particularly medium-sized clocks. He was good at it. Edmund King also had a hobby for which he was well known: gardening, on which he published two books in addition to his remarkable set of publications in comparative education.

Clearly, then, the methodology which Holmes constructed follows from his identity as a physicist and his concern with predictability? Similarly, King's concern with gardening permits us to understand his empathy for the complex interrelatedness of things – his concern with what he termed 'total cultural envelopes'? Perhaps – but there are two obvious problems with such hypotheses: the extrapolation from one aspect of personal biography to a definition of a specific form of comparative education is simplistic; and that kind of extrapolation does not cover the complexities of the relationship of Lauwerys with asparagus. (If Lauwerys had anything as trivial as a hobby, I am prepared to assert it was reading science fiction.)

Nevertheless, it is relatively easy to find statements about Holmes, originally trained as a physicist, and King the specialist in classics (Jones 1971; Trethewey 1976). Much of our interpretation of the kind of comparative education created by scholars concerned with 'method' proceeds by deduction from their 'disciplinary' identity; here meaning the kind of degree for which they had studied (in the English context, their undergraduate degree). Indeed, Andreas Kazamias, recently writing about himself as someone trained in history, emphasises this mode of interpretation and his role as an historian in the discussions of the 1960s (Kazamias 2009a, 2009b). The motif of intellectual identity also occurs in an exceptionally clear article by Brian Holmes (1981) about 'the models' which he and Edmund King used in comparative education. Holmes notes his own background as a physicist in contrast to King's background as a classicist. However, Holmes was clever enough to offer an immediate and perfectly proper mutation in the direction of the argument – the *causal* consequences of such differences are left unclear, although the interpretation remains firm: 'the models King uses, either implicitly or explicitly, are biological' (Holmes 1981, 155).[1]

Nevertheless, this emphasis on the biographical, on the intellectual ancestry of individual comparative education authors, and on the construction of the history of comparative education as an intellectual ascent from 'travellers' tales' towards 'a science', became routine. It was broadly repeated – despite a formal invitation to authors to stress the political and economic framings of the field of study – within Part One of the *International Handbook of Comparative Education* (Cowen and Kazamias 2009) (IHCEd). And the *International Handbook* version of the 'history' of comparative education drew in turn on Noah and Eckstein's classic text (1969); albeit with the addition of extra detail (Kaloyannaki and Kazamias 2009) that was part of the broader strategic effort by Kazamias in the two volumes of the IHCEd to show that there had been an historical voice within discussions of method in the 1960s.

Overall, the chapter narratives in the IHCEd continued to emphasise, like the text of Noah and Eckstein, academic work in the English language, post-Jullien; the voice in both accounts is mid-Atlantic; and the IHCEd continued to emphasise the *intellectual* trajectory of the academic study of comparative education, rather than trying to understand academic comparative education within the socio-economic and political pressures of the time-periods during which the work was written.

Unfortunately, an excessive emphasis on intellectual roots and lineages blocks other forms of historical interpretation[2] of the ideological positioning of the field of study in the 1960s (by several of its 'methodologists') as – more or less successfully – becoming scientific and as being properly and pragmatically concerned with policy; preferably both.

Thus, with this form of self-justification, we trap ourselves within an accumulation of errors. Three gross errors can be suggested, and any new 'history' of the field might wish to assess whether such errors, hypothesised here, are worthy of archival exploration and subsequent theoretical re-interpretation.

Errors?

One error is: dismissal. There are pleasures in reading historians writing about History: historians keep re-thinking it (Marwick 1970; Dahmus 1982; Munslow 1997; Doran 2013; Iriye 2013). The trouble with academic Comparative Education is that we do not. We are very busy people, with many broken things to mend before we sleep. As a consequence, 'our history' becomes over-simplified[3] and we became separated from the complexity of our roots, disjointedly wondering who we are – and where we should go next: Foucault or Derrida, economic globalisation or interculturality, peace and war or fragile states, more sociology or more history, social impact via contract research or better pedagogy for the Third World?

A second error – an over-emphasis on the useful and relevant – creates a strange quirk in our histories of ourselves. We retain in the periodisation of the 'intellectual history' which used to legitimate our academic selves, educational administrators such as Matthew Arnold and Victor Cousin, Kay-Shuttleworth and Horace Mann, Egerton Ryerson and Domingo Sarmiento; as if Lord Beveridge (after his work as a public servant in the UK on a Plan for a 'welfare state') was a British sociologist in the history of academic sociology or as if Franklin D. Roosevelt because of the New Deal should be named as a major economist in the history of economics in the USA. In other words, the teleology of our conventional version of ourselves (as a pragmatically useful science) leads to a category error. Certainly, the lineage of comparative education gains reflected glory for having in it the names of such reformers as the multi-talented Matthew Arnold and the brilliant Egerton Ryerson. That was the ideological point of including them in 'our' 1960s historical accounts: they were offered as heroes of administrative action and educational reform, looking overseas, pioneers in using a comparative vision – heroes who could later be used to legitimate academic comparative education, in one phase of its existence, as useful.

However, by labelling Horace Mann or Sarmiento as 'comparative educationists', any distinction between comparative education as a field of study in the university and as 'applied comparative education' (illustrated not only by the work of nineteenth-century educational administrators but also by World Bank proposals for the reform of education) is glossed over; an error which is politically serious by the time you try to classify PISA as a form of comparative education when it is clear it is also a form of transnational educational governance and a signifier of new patterns in the flow of international power (Moss and Goldstein 2014; Cowen 2014a; Auld and Morris 2016; Morris 2016; Adamson et al. 2017; Komatsu and Rappleye 2017.)

The third error, a *reductio ad absurdum*, is simple. The argument that comparative education is defined by (or, at the very least, distinguished by) its method was always uninspiring even in the 1960s when it reached its ideological apogee. These days – when the quality of PhD theses in educational studies in England is more and more defined by the explicitness of the methods of empirical research which are used rather than the intellectual complexity, subtlety, and interpretative power of the thesis text (Cowen 2012, 2016a) – it becomes urgent to question the banality that the major characteristic of comparative education is method.

The question is vital – not merely because of the urge, itself ideological, to distinguish the academic territory of comparative education with its presumed 'special methods' from sociology, or history. It is also vital because emphasising and prioritising method is to empty a field of study of any significance other than the worship of proper technical procedures. Craft skills are indeed important; but good plumbers and good medical doctors serve higher goals than their skill sets. We do too.

At least the mirage of a magic method forces us – sooner or later – to ask of the archives and of ourselves: what are our past and present forms of comparative education and how can you define 'form'? Then, perhaps, we can contemplate new styles of academic comparative education which avoid the vacuity of the word 'international' and the laziness of assuming that the world can now be referred to, non-problematically, as 'globalised'. Anxiety about method has constrained much of our past. It should not be permitted to constrain our future. However, if we do not ask 'What did you do in the Methods Wars, Daddy?' then what other question can be put to the archives and the corpus of work in the 1960s?

Moving on?

Granted that some rewriting of the classic version of 'our history' has already occurred, it is becoming easier to suggest that our assumptions about the conventional history of English-language comparative education will be made more complex – and might at some point be carefully rewritten – by asking less about the methodologies and more about the 'readings of the global' in the work of various scholars in the 1960s.

When I first invented the phrase 'reading the global' (Cowen 2000), it was intended to specify and confirm one of the basic and permanent tasks of academic comparative education: always to be defining and re-defining the political, economic, and social worlds in which it was working and to be clear about what (indeed, almost literally, how far) it wanted to 'see', especially inter-nationally or transnationally. My irritation at the time was partly linked to the ways in which the expression 'globalisation' was swamping the literature of 'comparative education'; even though, when I first invented the term 'reading the global', I was also thinking about a comparative education which might analyse aristocratic forms of education within, say, the city states of Machiavelli's Italy, or a comparative education which could de-code patterns of education in a Latin American world long dominated by Spanish political, economic, religious, and cultural colonisation; or educational provision within a British Empire that construed education in politically

different ways in Canada, in East Africa, in the West Indian islands, and in the Indian penin-
sula. By the time I returned to the expression (Cowen 2009a), my interest was still to break
comparative education out of its post-1817 concerns with the reform of nineteenth-
century and twentieth-century modes of 'mass' schooling, to escape the straitjacket of
'normal puzzle' comparative education: the reform of *sectors* of educational systems
that are of policy interest to administrators (such as the descendants of Mann and
Ryerson and Sarmiento).

One definition of 'reading the global' is 'the selection of an agenda of academic attention, the naming of anxieties and puzzles embedded in an interpretation of those foreign
parts of the world which are "seen", in the sense that those places are deliberately raised to
visibility' (Cowen 2009b, 337). Longer definitions are possible (Cowen 2016b, 46–48). The
theme remained visible – my anxiety is clearly continuous – in something a little different I
wrote, in a footnote, about three years ago. I had asserted:

> We have never sorted out the relations between changes in the field of study and the four
> 'spaces' that almost all comparative educationists occupy – their remembered spaces of
> origin, crudely their sense of their nationalities; their spaces of professional experience,
> crudely where their university is; thirdly, which regions or 'countries' they address in their
> work; and fourthly, the international political space which they seek to interpret. (Cowen
> 2014a, 295)

It is salutary to be skewered by one's own footnotes, but the *aperçu* about the international politics of space is routinely, almost axiomatically and permanently, made relevant because of 'outsiders' within the field of comparative education.

Embodied outsiders

The academic field of study known as comparative education had a lot of 'outsiders' in it
and it still has. Early outsiders, as university comparative education took shape, included
Nicholas Hans, Isaac Kandel, and Robert Ulich. By the 1950s, George Bereday and
Joseph Lauwerys were becoming well known in their academic roles in Teachers
College, Columbia University, and the Institute of Education. The tradition is still alive
both in the comparative education sections of Teachers' College New York (Gita Steiner-
Khamsi) and in London where there has been a sequence in area skills that cover Scandi-
navia (through Jon Lauglo, then Susanne Wiborg) though the pattern is much broader:
illustratively Stavros Moutsios and Steve Carney in Denmark, Terri Kim and Michele
Schweisfurth in the United Kingdom, and Jeremy Rappleye and Ed Vickers in Japan.
Terri Kim herself (2014) has covered the theme of this kind of 'outsider' academic mobility
in comparative education. A current and comprehensive listing would be remarkable and
would stretch from identifying (as specialists in comparative education) Germans working
in Sweden (e.g. Barbara Schulte) to Japanese working in Australia (e.g. Keita Takayama).
The tradition in the field is an old one and a strong one; and a good one.

A good one? What is the intellectual point in having 'outsiders' in the field of study? The
traditional point is obvious: if you are going to appoint an academic to specialise in Eastern
European education, a good candidate might be a Pole, who spoke several other
languages besides Polish (e.g. Janusz Tomiak, formerly of the Institute of Education and
the School of East European and Slavonic Studies in the University of London). Or if you
were seeking to build a comparative education department in London in 1948, you

might choose a person of Belgian origin, who spoke several languages, who had already made his reputation as an educator – both as a school teacher and as a specialist in the teaching of science within the UK – and who was brilliantly networked for comparative purposes: for example if he had worked, as Lauwerys did, with R.A. Butler and with the Committee of Allied Ministers of Education in Exile in London during the Second World War.

However, oddly enough, the outsider may be constructed by the parochialism of insiders.

Grant

Such a case is that of Nigel Grant who – born in Glasgow, growing up in Inverness, based as an academic in Edinburgh and then in Glasgow – was very alert to the Englishness of much English comparative education. He complained steadily and publicly about the carelessness with which the phrase 'English education' was used to mean education in the United Kingdom of Great Britain and Northern Ireland; and about the bad habit of speakers at conferences – not merely in the USA; also in the UK – who kept referring to 'British education' when there is no such thing. His outsiderness grew stronger as he grew older: he developed a very serious commitment to Scottish nationalism. Nigel Grant also captures the theme of 'remembered spaces of origin' – notably the Scottish Highlands – and he had a sharp sense of 'a space of professional experience': teacher colleges and universities in Scotland. A very good Special Issue of *Comparative Education* put together by Nigel's friend Thyge Winther-Jensen (2000b), traces most of these themes and many others: see especially Winther-Jensen's 'Notes and Comments' (2000a, 127–128) for a sketch of Nigel Grant's career.

Here, however, the core point is Grant's 'reading of the global'. He saw, among other places (which for obvious reasons included Canada) 'the Celtic fringe': he had an interest in the languages of Scotland, Ireland, Wales, and Cornwall, as well as Brittany (Sutherland 2000). His concern with 'identity' led him to a personal friendship with Jagdish Gundara (2000) Head of the International Centre for Intercultural Studies in the University of London Institute of Education and Grant wrote a flurry of articles in which he specifically addressed 'intercultural education' (1997).

Grant's empathy stretched north rather than south – he retained, perhaps later even cultivating, a slight sense of England as 'the auld enemy'. (The term is used contemporaneously to capture the rivalry of a traditional inter-nation soccer match but it has deeper and even more violent roots.) Nigel Grant looked north: he extended his personal and professional gaze (his 'reading of the global') to Scandinavia, especially the Denmark of his personal friend Professor Thyge Winther-Jensen.

Of course, he was also interested in whichever country he happened to be in: I travelled with him in several countries including Spain and Egypt and Denmark. I remember him reading Lorca in Madrid, practising his Arabic by the Nile, and his Danish in a hamburger restaurant.

But his work contains a slight puzzle. It is almost – but not quite true – that the fourth theme (which 'international political space' did he seek to interpret?) was framed by the fact that his gaze went to the east rather than to the west. His doctoral thesis was on Eastern Europe and became a book (1969) and his classic text (1964) about education in the USSR became a widely read paperback which went through numerous editions between 1964 and 1979. However, this is where the theme gets to be interesting: I get no sense that he was particularly alert to international political space.

There was nothing in Grant's work or political philosophy which frames a left-wing Glaswegian interpretation of the virtues of socialist societies and the proletariat. Even though King writes of Grant's 'special insights into revolutionary countries' (King 2000 , 129), King is not emphasising the theme of 'revolution', but the similarity of his own 'culturalist' interests and his concern with human detail to the interests of Grant; though Grant of course wrote far more on minorities.

Grant's gaze going eastwards was not because he was a socialist revolutionary or because he wished to locate his comparative education as a contribution to understanding the shaping of the young as 'the political young' or to trace the educational competition that was part of the Cold War itself. Grant looked eastwards because he had already chosen to have access to those languages. I was surprised to learn (via a formal and professional note of enquiry to Thyge Winther-Jensen) that Grant's knowledge of Russian did not come from the training in foreign languages offered in the British Armed Forces. (Grant was in an artillery regiment – at the time of the Cold War, the UK had compulsory military service for two years.) Grant, as a person, was clearly fascinated by languages – in the plural, as it were. His Master's degree work was based on reflections about 'traditional Asian scripts as vehicles of mass education' (Winther-Jensen 2000a, 127). His languages were a hobby, pursued regularly with the energy and conviction that Lauwerys occasionally accorded to his asparagus. And it was languages rather than a sense of the international politics of space which sent his gaze eastwards for two of his major books; his other major book writing, according to the Bibliography provided by Winther-Jensen (2000b, 245–251), being about Scotland and Scottish education within Britain.

It was Grant's alertness to identities, especially, the identities of minorities and their existence in specific places and the struggle to maintain and strengthen their identity in place and over time, which gave and gives life to his comparative education. His comparative education is not about 'borrowing' and 'transfer'; but about some of the necessary stabilities and immobilities of identity and the difficulties of survival of minorities within larger nations or political units – including both the USSR and the new political identity of Europe. That new identity of Europe led directly to identity decisions taken in a referendum in Scotland and to Brexit shock in the later referendum in the UK. Grant's 'agenda of attention' continues to be fruitful.

Lauwerys

Unlike Grant, Joseph Lauwerys committed himself explicitly to a statement of his own value position. This was published in a book by A. V. Judges on philosophies of education and, in one of its chapters, Lauwerys (1957a) sketched his position as 'a scientific humanist'. The immediate relationship of this view of a secular world (Lauwerys was born into a Catholic family) to Lauwerys' 'reading of the global' is not immediately apparent until the social and political frame of the post-1945 world is remembered.

Lauwerys (with his commitment to science, to the value of human beings, to 'education' in the sense of distribution of reliable knowledge and his strong orientation towards social action which his view of 'scientific humanism' included) became involved, very early, in assisting in the invention of that post-war world. Within Europe he was – even during the Second World War – deeply involved in post-war reconstruction. As indicated earlier, he worked closely with the Allied Ministers of Education in Exile. Thus, he knew personally many of the Ministers of Education in the post-war period (a network quite important for the future of the Comparative Education Society in Europe). The wartime work also helped to define concerns that immediately informed the (World) *Yearbooks of Education* from 1948, which were co-edited with various persons, including George Bereday. Lauwerys' second major involvement in the reconstruction of post-war world was via UNESCO for whom he was a consultant in the early years 1945 to 1948. The third illustration of his involvement in efforts aimed at the reconstruction of the post-war world and the recovery of democracy was a remarkable set of lectures which he gave in Japan after the war: lectures published in both Japanese and English to the title *Morals, democracy and education* (Lauwerys 1957b) and which led to a lifelong friendship with Professor M. Hiratsuka. More generally, his international travels were remarkable and included Africa, China, and Latin America – as well of course as continental Europe and the USA (McLean 1981).

A sense of the scale and complexity of his achievements can be gained from his 'author note' which he provided for a book about The Atlantic Institute of Education, in Halifax, Nova Scotia:

> Joseph A. Lauwerys, D.Sc. (Ghent), D.Litt. (London), F.R.I.C, Commandeur des Palmes Académiques. Director Emeritus, Atlantic Institute of Education. Professor Emeritus in the University of London. President, International Montessori Association and Vice-Chairman, Unesco Conciliation and Good Offices Commission. Formerly Dean of the Faculty of Education, University of London, and Chairman of the Department of Comparative Education. Consultant to Unesco, 1945–1948. Joint Editor, *World Year Book of Education*, 1948–1970. Professor at the Sorbonne, 1969–1971. (Anderson and Lauwerys 1978)

Lauwerys 'reading of the global' was that of a practical consultant. He not only advised on education in Africa, but also on education in Chile and in Brazil. His advisory work in Chile and in Brazil was not, of course, concerned with post-war reconstruction but with university and science policy in Chile, and with teacher education in Brazil. Rather surprisingly, he visited Brazil nine times in a period when he was, if anything, rather more visible and famous in Chile.

This remarkable range of practical activity, which included a very wide range of overseas lecturing and networking (e.g. with the Rockefeller Foundation in New York and making links with Teachers' College Columbia) can be understood in terms of Lauwerys' view of the point and purpose of Comparative Education. The good comparativist would be concerned with but not fixated about methodology, nor about a scientific approach in Comparative Education. The good comparativist would be concerned with 'educational statesmanship'. This is a fascinating concept. The Lectures on 'education morals and democracy' (1957) re-read in 2017 leave a strong impression of very clear intellectual organisation and sequence (and a considerable knowledge of the economic and political bases of the Greek *polis* in classical Greece); but it is the tone which is fascinating: gentleness, exploration, persuasion. When I first read them as a student in 1967 I termed them 'wise'. (This was not a correct answer in an MA seminar devoted to 'method' in comparative education.)

It was also Lauwerys' vision of education statesmanship which – partly – framed the conception of CESE which took shape in the very early 60's in meetings in London and in Amsterdam. Lauwerys saw CESE not so much as an academic society devoted to the creation of a scientific comparative education nor as a society which through the Election of Members would create an elite of experts. He saw the Society as a particular formation of the best and brightest, the most mature and experienced academic specialists in education in Europe who through deliberations and permanent 'conversation' might be able to offer wisdom about educational policy to Ministers of Education across Europe. His call was for energy, commitment to change, strong disputation, and always a sense of evidence. (Lauwerys, being a polymath, was formally qualified in biology and in chemistry and also had a BSc. in 'special physics'.)

Thus, although he was not in any anxious or continual way concerned with 'method' and especially not rules of method in research derived from his first set of bachelor degrees in the sciences, Lauwerys – like so many of the early comparativists such as Hans who complained strongly about difficulties of getting statistics – was very committed to the careful collection of data (including reliable statistics) and he was influential through UNESCO in encouraging this.

There was another continuity from his first identity as a scientist and as a science educator which affected his view of international political space. Lauwerys' particular dislike (once expressed in personal correspondence with the author of this article while we were both working in North America) was autarky. He disliked not being open to the world and in this sense he identified with the academic society and networks of the community of natural scientists in which he had taken his original educational formation. Not unlike Karl Popper, he was convinced that habits of collecting evidence, habits of open discussion, and habits of international exchange of ideas and information were in themselves a form of democracy and an edging towards 'the educational statesmanship' to which comparative educationists in their academic societies should aspire. He was, for example, also very deeply committed to the New Education Fellowship and its efforts to create international understanding and to a wide range of educational tours, which were finally extended to the USSR and which were later taken up and run very well by Brian Holmes (until 1985).[4]

Lauwerys' characteristics – his charisma, his lecturing style, and his ability as a writer and as a BBC broadcaster (notably on science and science education) to express complex ideas with great clarity – are fairly well known, and are not the point of closure here. The point is that he saw international political space (and comparative education) as arenas for action and for acting out a view of citizenship of the world. The vision he offered – and to a remarkable extent could deliver in terms of consultancies and relations with Teachers College and the Rockefeller foundation – was 'educational statesmanship'. Fascinatingly nebulous as a concept, it is pleasing that no one has yet invented a managerial training course in it. There is an alternative: well-taught courses in comparative education which develop a sharp sense of history, sociological analytical power, anthropological sensitivity, and a very clear alertness to international political space. All our best courses do that.[5]

Holmes and King

Brian Holmes was very much of the Institute of Education and for a very great deal of his career a very energetic part of it, first as an Assistant Editor to the *Yearbook of Education* from 1953 and finally as Dean of the Faculty of Education of the University of London and one of the Pro-Directors of the Institute – an important policy advising position (McLean 1987). Edmund King also delighted in his own institution which was King's College, London. Part of his considerable charm was the gleeful pleasure which he took in referring to himself as King of King's and he would rehearse at appropriate moments the historical links of King's College to some of the major figures in British literary life. He often spoke fondly of his office which had a view of the Thames. (One can hardly blame him – the Institute of Education building looks magnificent from the outside but it is not a pleasant building for human beings to work in during the summer. Or indeed the winter.) Of course, both Holmes and King overlapped in their teaching and in departmental duties in the Institute, where MA teaching plans and examination papers and so on were rehearsed under a variety of Professors after Lauwerys. (There was no overlap at PhD level; both scholars were free to supervise in the way they thought fit and there was no common doctoral seminar.)

Their interest in specific countries varied somewhat – though their teaching duties over the years meant alternate-year teaching of a course on the USA and another course on France.

Holmes' interest in particular countries included the USA, Japan, and the USSR. Encouraged by Lauwerys, Holmes spent time as a Visiting Professor in the USA and he developed an interest in John Dewey. Partly as a consequence of what would now be called 'study-leave' residence in the USA and his strong interest in Dewey, he lectured far more comfortably on the USA than he did on France. One of Holmes (1965a) best pieces of writing was a serious and sustained account of the thinking of John Dewey in the book by Nash, Kazamias, and Perkinson. Other good writing about a specific place, which achieves a considerable level of intensity and interest, is his account of moral education in Japan – a chapter in his book *Problems of Education* (Holmes 1965b). The third geographic area of the world that was for Holmes an area of sustained interest was the Soviet Union. The Institute Tour was a matter of considerable pride and pleasure for Brian Holmes not least because it embraced the principle of 'scientists talking to scientists' but also because it appealed, in my judgment, to Brian Holmes the teacher. He was a brilliant seminar teacher and tutor. For many who went on the Tours the visit was a cathartic experience and Holmes could, as a teacher, see the intense moments of 'comparative' learning that many of the Tour members experienced during each visit.

King's country-specific interests were loosely linked to knowledge of Latin and Greek and a sense of the civilisations of Rome and Greece. This gave him a particular empathy with Spain, Italy, and to some extent France. His earlier work on adult and lifelong education, a specialisation before his career in comparative education itself, had meant visits to Denmark, the USA, the USSR, and 'three other' Eastern European countries (King 2000, 131). Of course, as a Board Member and then later as Editor of the journal *Comparative Education*, his general range of 'area knowledge' was wide and grew steadily wider. Similarly, Holmes as someone who had been involved from 1953 in the preparation of the annual *Yearbook of Education* (published by Evans Brothers) also had considerable area knowledge outside of his formal lecturing responsibilities and his personal interests. Holmes' general range of 'area knowledge' also grew steadily wider – he graduated over 100 doctoral candidates in his career. Thus, as specialist comparative educationists, they both knew some places well, they both had travelled a lot especially within continental Europe, and they both had enjoyed visits to Japan.

One crucial difference was, however, in their 'reading of the global'

Holmes' 'reading of the global' was peculiarly corroded by his methodology. Certainly, it was the case that he could construe a doctoral thesis for one of his students on Algeria, Brazil, China, Egypt, Greece, Iran, Japan, Mexico, the Sudan, or Venezuela, without any intellectual strain. However, his definition of a 'problem' was slightly idiosyncratic: it was without a view of the global. His definition of a 'problem' included permitting an individual scholar to decide a topic was 'a problem'. (That topic could become a Holmesian problem by a technique of specifying tightly *one* particular change which upset a previous equilibrium.) The only generic frame of a problem which he offered was again idiosyncratic. The most generic source of problems was a series of 'explosions': of population, of expectations, and of knowledge (Holmes 1965b, 36–38).

In other words, his 'reading of the global' was so generalised as to permit his problems to float in de-politicised space. There is, in his published comparative education work, no sustained interpretation of the Cold War, of the relationship between major powers such as the USA and Latin America, the USSR and East Europe, or of the British and India, or Africa.

Granted that his methodology addressed the classic and contemporary theme of 'transfer', he developed no theory of international political or economic relations which framed either his theory or the practice of transfer. Indeed, in the first part of his magnum opus (Holmes 1965b, 9–11), he writes to the concept of 'cultural borrowing' (and then to the concept of 'selective cultural borrowing') – a peculiarly anodyne and vague labelling of the world which precisely hides the politics of power and international transfer.

His comparative education was rooted in notions of pragmatic 'problem-solving', with a sociology drawn particularly from structural functionalist models which he sketches in his *tour de force* 'Paradigm Shifts in Comparative Education' (Holmes 1986). His 'reading of the global' edges towards a technology of intended improvement, very much influenced by the thinking of Robert King-Hall which in turn had been refined in the Gulf of Arabia. Paradoxically, this version of 'reading the global' helped to shape Holmes' mid-Atlantic rather technocratic comparative education which (despite Holmes' role in CESE for over two decades) was largely uninfluenced by European assumptions about the uses of the intellect.

In contrast, King's 'reading of the global' was a reading which absorbed and offered up a great deal of serious information (about history, economics, and so on) but he lurches most uneasily not simply into cultural detail but into simplistic, journalistic, cultural detail. His chapter on the USA in his classic text *Other Schools and Ours* contains wondrous generalisations of the kind: 'School is still a sort of oasis, a happy land shielded from the stresses and competitions of adult life – a children's garden in more senses than Froebel ... ' (King 1973, 271). Fortunately, I read an earlier edition of his text when I was a student – by 1972 my own children were in school in the USA and I was teaching some extremely bright students in the State University of New York at Buffalo. My experience there was pleasurably challenging, and fortunately not covered by King's generalisation: 'Foreign professors generally find American students too docile for their taste – a surprising thing in the land of liberty' (King 1973, 305). (It will be recalled that in the early 1970s the land of the free was busy freeing itself and its 'children' from Vietnam in very difficult domestic political circumstances.) Yes, the fluency of his writing was remarkable and readily understandable; but even if the very considerable text of the fourth edition was partly achieved with the help of a tape recorder, it is salutary to re-read his opening sentences on the first of his 'case studies' (Denmark): 'The flags are almost certain to be flying today in Denmark. Soon after we see the green copper crowns of tower and steeple and the clean warmth of … ' (King 1973, 77). Probably Edmund King meets well enough the label 'culturalist' which Bill Halls (1973) used to typify much of British comparative education in this period.

At least King's 'reading of the global', unlike that of Brian Holmes, included time-past. Among his many editing endeavours, he revised William Boyd's classic *History of Western Education* (1965). However, somewhat like Holmes, his sense of sociological thinking was weak, he largely ignored (for analytical purposes) the major sociologists of the nineteenth century, and his 'reading of the global' was jejune: his intellectual apparatus ('newness', 'the [contraceptive] pill', 'the computer chip') loosely coupled with concepts such as 'cultural envelopes' got him into great intellectual difficulties. Erwin Epstein (1986) gives a thoughtful analysis of the row with Margaret Scotford Archer (1979) when she chose to respond in print to a critical review by King of her own book *The Social Origins of Educational Systems*.

In this form of academic deafness (to sociology), King was very similar to Brian Holmes. Holmes, astonishingly, used the philosopher Popper to create a sociology (more precisely a typology of potential sources of disequilibria) which distinguished between normative propositions open to debate and change, institutional patterns strongly framed by 'sociological laws', and environmental circumstances. These were captured in Holmes' famous three circles (of norms, institutions, and a borrowing from Hans of 'environmental circumstances'). The irony was that, at the same time, Holmes used a very pragmatic definition of problem-solving by John Dewey to frame the philosophy and typology of action which informed his methodology.

This is all in sharp contrast to Lauwerys who was well and widely read in terms of thinkers such as John Stuart Mill and John Locke and also in terms of history. Surprisingly this included not only the political and cultural history of Latin America, of the Low Countries, and Scandinavia but, also, his sense of the economic history of Britain since the industrial revolution was acute. Lauwerys' major gift was his encyclopaedic abilities that permitted him to talk and empathise with Karl Mannheim on the one hand and Otto Neurath on the other.

Conclusion

The broadest version of the perspective behind this article is that the allegedly well-known history of comparative education could be more sharply interpreted by reviewing the relationships between individual biography, professional work places (universities of the period) and personal 'readings of the global' in the work of individual scholars as they responded to political and social worlds outside of the university. In principle, these probably affected how they utilised the epistemic traditions in which they were trained and also influenced the new kinds of comparative education they aspired to write.

The significance of the phrase 'reading the global' is that it implies a classification of the political, sociological, and economic world – notably the international or transnational world – into what is seen and what is not seen; what will be taken as important and what may not even be noticed. The implications – subject to detailed demonstration by archival research – could be considerable. There are implications for how the subject of comparative education is taught. For example, when I was being introduced to comparative education in the (University of London) Institute of Education, the basic pedagogic assumption was that if students knew the principles and practices of American, English, French, German, and Soviet patterns of education, we were well on the way to 'understanding' most of the educational systems in the world. Similarly, 'reading the global' in a particular way can define the actions which should be taken in the name of 'comparative and international education' (Cowen 2006; Crossley and Watson 2011; Epstein 2016).

However, the strategic orientation of the article was simpler than these complexities – largely the point is: in what ways might new questions be generated and taken to 'the archives'.

It can be suggested that all forms of comparative education have at least four motifs: their agenda of attention; their agenda of approach; an agenda of action and – because often it is necessary for academics to make alliances if their voices are to be heard outside of the academy – their agenda of agglutination. Of course, how to deal with asparagus can be construed in approximately the same way, but the answers for comparative education are perhaps more complex.

For comparative education, at least three of the agendas (and I am fairly confident all do – even 'the method' bit) have moral dimensions, and carry also *sub-rasa* assumptions about democracy, citizenship, the social role of knowledge, and so on. However, if the 'agenda of approach' is here taken as a synonym of method, then the prior questions become: what do you 'see'? What are your 'hot topics' or, in a different and more dignified vocabulary, your 'normal puzzles'?

The argument that has been offered so far is that agendas of attention are crucially shaped by 'readings of the global' and not merely by what 'approach' is stated as the permanent 'best way' (Kazamias' historical approach; King's cultural envelopes; Holmes' problem-solving methods).

What then, was Hans' 'reading of the global' – his reading of international political spaces? That is not the same as being able to construe most nations of the world through his 'factors'. And in what way does Hans' reading of international political space permit an agenda of possible action? Are the 'factors' forms of very powerful domestic immunologies (against 'foreign infections' – which might or might not be 'cultural borrowings')? What did Hans say about that and did he anticipate (as clearly Lauwerys did) alliances and political links ('agendas of agglutination' with for example Foundations) that could make things happen? Do the archives tell us?

It would be nice to know; but that is hardly the core point. Perhaps the core point is muddle. We now have major and politically powerful forms of 'applied comparative education'. Assume that we have a world conventionally characterised by the word 'globalisation'. And assume that within an area of work rather carelessly called 'international education', we have a plethora of moral visions, international humanitarian interventions, state rebuilding, the rescuing of refugees and their education, and lots of other bits and pieces of earnest educational action overseas.

How then, within comparative education, do we 'see' that world in way that permits us to bear historic witness and reveal its new forms of 'imperium'? Paradoxically that involves looking backwards and asking of the archives what is missing, or not yet revealed, in earlier efforts to grasp the remarkable complexities and modalities of 'transfer' and shape-shifting as – themselves (Cowen 2009b, 2014b, 2018) – expressions of international power.

Notes

1. The refusal of a causal relationship was wise. Lauwerys sometimes praised King's books on gardening and Lauwerys' own first degree was in biology; but he would not have been amused to be carelessly grafted by Holmes onto the intellectual world of Edmund J. King.
2. Yes, the 'history of comparative education' has been updated since Noah and Eckstein (1969) and the *International Handbook of Comparative Education* (2009) – notably in the work of Maria Manzon (2011). There are also alternative 'histories of comparative education'; including a brilliant short essay by Nóvoa and Yariv-Mashal (2003). The theme of my own article, here, on embodied comparative education is that this re-thinking should continue; not least by sorting out some fresh questions for assessment through archival research.
3. Robin Shields in his textbook *Globalization and International Education* (2013) summarises the history of the field in two pages.
4. In January 1991, after the attack by Soviet paratroops on the main radio and TV station in Latvia, I cancelled the Tour; and did not re-start it.
5. There is some evidence to indicate this happy assertion may be over-confident (Kubow and Blosser 2016).

Disclosure statement

No potential conflict of interest was reported by the author.

References

Adamson, B., K. Forestier, P. Morris, and C. Han. 2017. "PISA, Policymaking and Political Pantomime: Education Policy Referencing Between England and Hong Kong." *Comparative Education* 53 (2): 192–208.

Anderson, G. J., and J. A. Lauwerys. 1978. *Institutional Leadership for Educational Reforms: The Atlantic Institute of Education*. Paris: UNESCO.

Archer, M. S. 1979. *Social Origins of Educational Systems*. London: Sage.

Auld, E., and P. Morris. 2016. "PISA, Policy and Persuasion: Translating Complex Conditions into Education 'Best Practice'." *Comparative Education* 52 (2): 202–229.

Boyd, W. 1965. *The History of Western Education*. 7th ed. Revised and enlarged by E. J. King. New York: Barnes and Noble.

Cowen, R. 2000. "Comparing Futures or Comparing Pasts?" *Comparative Education* 36 (3): 333–342.

Cowen, R. 2006. "Acting Comparatively Upon the Educational World: Puzzles and Possibilities." *Oxford Review of Education* 32 (5): 561–573.

Cowen, R. 2009a. "Editorial Introduction: The National, the International and the Global." In *International Handbook of Comparative Education*, edited by R. Cowen and A. M. Kazamias, 337–340. Dordrecht: Springer.

Cowen, R. 2009b. "The Transfer, Translation and Transformation of Educational Processes: And Their Shape-shifting?" *Comparative Education* 45 (3): 315–327.

Cowen, R. 2012. "Robustly Researching the Relevant: A Note on Creation Myths in Comparative Education." In *Enlightenment, Creativity and Education: Polities, Politics, Performances*, edited by L. Wikander, C. Gustaffson, and U. Riis, 3–26. Rotterdam: Sense Publishers & CESE.

Cowen, R. 2014a. "Ways of Knowing, Outcomes, and 'Comparative Education': Be Careful What You Pray For." *Comparative Education* 50 (3): 282–301.

Cowen, R. 2014b. "With the Exception of Switzerland … Thoughts About the Nation and Educational Research." *International Journal for the Historiography of Education* 2: 216–222.

Cowen, R. 2016a. "Doctoring the Doctorate in England." In *Knowledge Society and Doctoral Studies: Research, Education and Training in a New Landscape*, edited by D. Palomba and C. Cappa, 81–116. Rome: Aracne.

Cowen, R. 2016b. "Comparative Education and Intercultural Education: What Are the Questions?." In *Establishing a Culture of Intercultural Education: Essays and Papers in Honour of Jagdish Gundara*, edited by L. Bash and D. Coulby, 41–60. Cambridge: Cambridge Scholars.

Cowen, R. 2018. "Narrating and Relating Educational Reform and Comparative Education." In *Critical Analyses of Educational Reform in an Era of Transnational Governance*, edited by E. Hultqvist, S. Lindblad, and T. Popkewitz, 23–39. Dordrecht: Springer.

Cowen, R., and A. M. Kazamias, eds. 2009. *International Handbook of Comparative Education*. Dordrecht: Springer.

Crossley, M., and K. Watson. 2011. "Comparative and International Education: Policy Transfer, Context Sensibility and Professional Development." In *Disciplines of Education: Their Role in the Future of Education Research*, edited by J. Furlong and M. Lawn, 103–121. London: Routledge, Taylor and Francis Group.

Dahmus, J. 1982. *Seven Medieval Historians*. Chicago: Nelson-Hall.

Doran, R., ed. 2013. *Philosophy of History After Hayden White*. London: Bloomsbury.

Epstein, E. H. 1986. "Currents Left and Right: Ideology in Comparative Education." In *New Approaches to Comparative Education*, edited by P. G. Altbach and G. P. Kelly, 233–259. Chicago: The University of Chicago Press.

Epstein, E. H. 2016. "Why Comparative and International Education? Reflections on the Conflation of Names." In *Teaching Comparative Education: Trends and Issues Informing Practice*, edited by P. K. Kubow and A. H. Blosser, 57–73. Oxford: Symposium Books.

Grant, N. 1964. *Soviet Education*. Harmondsworth: Penguin.

Grant, N. 1969. *Schools, Society and Progress in Eastern Europe*. Oxford: Pergamon Press.

Grant, N. 1997. "Intercultural Education in the UK." In *World Yearbook of Education: Intercultural Education*, edited by D. Coulby, C. Jones, and J. Gundara, 178–190. London: Kogan Page.

Gundara, J. 2000. "Issues of Discrimination in European Educational Systems." *Comparative Education* 36 (2): 223–234.

Halls, W. D. 1973. "Culture and Education: The Culturalist Approach to Comparative Education." In *Relevant Methods in Comparative Education*, edited by R. Edwards, B. Holmes, and J. v. de Graff, 119–135. Hamburg: UNESCO Institute for Education.

Holmes, B. 1965a. "The Reflective Man: John Dewey." In *The Educated Man: Studies in the History of Educational Thought*, edited by P. Nash, A. M. Kazamias, and H. Perkinson, 304–334. New York: John Wiley and Sons.

Holmes, B. 1965b. *Problems in Education: A Comparative Approach*. London: Routledge & Kegan Paul.

Holmes, B. 1981. "Models in Comparative Education." *Compare: A Journal of Comparative and International Education* 11 (2): 155–161.

Holmes, B. 1986. "Paradigm Shifts in Comparative Education." In *New Approaches to Comparative Education*, edited by P. G. Altbach and G. P. Kelly, 179–199. Chicago: The University of Chicago Press.

Iriye, A. 2013. *Global and Transnational History: The Past, Present and Future*. London: Palgrave Macmillan.

Jones, P. E. 1971. *Comparative Education: Purpose and Method*. St. Lucia: University of Queensland Press.

Kaloyannaki, P., and A. M. Kazamias. 2009. "The Modernist Beginnings of Comparative Education: The Proto-Scientific and the Reformist-Meliorist Administrative Motif." In *International Handbook of Comparative Education*, edited by R. Cowen and A. M. Kazamias, 11–36. Dordrecht: Springer.

Kazamias, A. M. 2009a. "Forgotten Men, Forgotten Themes: The Historical-Philosophical-Cultural and Liberal Humanist Motif in Comparative Education." In *International Handbook of Comparative Education*, edited by R. Cowen and A. M. Kazamias, 37–58. Dordrecht: Springer.

Kazamias, A. M. 2009b. "Reclaiming a Lost Legacy: The Historical Humanist Vision in Comparative Education." In *International Handbook of Comparative Education*, edited by R. Cowen and A. M. Kazamias, 1267–1276. Dordrecht: Springer.

Kim, T. 2014. "The Intellect, Mobility and Epistemic Positioning in Doing Comparisons and Comparative Education." *Comparative Education* 50 (1): 58–72.

King, E. J. 1973. *Other Schools and Ours: Comparative Studies for Today*. 4th ed. London: Holt Rinehart and Winston.

King, E. 2000. "Nigel Grant's Contribution to Comparative Education." *Comparative Education* 36 (2): 129–133.

Komatsu, H., and J. Rappleye. 2017. "A New Global Policy Regime Founded on Invalid Statistics? Hanushek, Woessmann, PISA and Economic Growth." *Comparative Education* 53 (2): 166–191.

Kubow, P. K., and A. H. Blosser. 2016. *Teaching Comparative Education: Trends and Issues Informing Practice*. Oxford: Symposium Books.

Lauwerys, J. A. 1957a. "Scientific Humanism." In *Education and the Philosophic Mind*, edited by A. V. Judges, 142–166. London: Harrap.

Lauwerys, J. A. 1957b. *Morals, Democracy and Education*. Tokyo: Institute for Democratic Education.

Manzon, M. 2011. *Comparative Education: The Construction of a Field*. Hong Kong/Dordrecht: Comparative Education Research Centre. The University of Hong Kong/Springer.

Marwick, A. 1970. *The Nature of History*. London: Macmillan.

McLean, M., ed. 1981. *Joseph A. Lauwerys: A Festchrift*. London: University of London, Institute of Education Library.

McLean, M., ed. 1987. "Editorial." *Compare: A Journal of Comparative and International Education* 17 (1): 3–6.

Morris, P. 2016. "Education Policy, Cross-national Tests of Pupil Achievement, and the Pursuit of World-class Schooling: A Critical Analysis." *An Inaugural Professorial Lecture*. London: UCL Institute of Education Press.

Moss, G., and H. Goldstein eds. 2014. "Special Issue (49): Knowledge in Numbers." *Comparative Education* 50 (3).

Munslow, A. 1997. *Deconstructing History*. London: Routledge.

Noah, H. J., and M. A. Eckstein. 1969. *Toward a Science of Comparative Education*. New York: Macmillan.

Nóvoa, A., and T. Yariv-Mashal. 2003. "Comparative Research in Education: A Mode of Governance or a Historical Journey?" *Comparative Education* 39 (4): 423–438.

Shields, R. 2013. *Globalization and International Education*. London: Bloomsbury.

Sutherland, M. B. 2000. "Problems of Diversity in Policy and Practice: Celtic Languages in the United Kingdom." *Comparative Education* 36 (2): 199–209.

Trethewey, A. R. 1976. *Introducing Comparative Education*. Rushcutters Bay: Pergamon Press.

Winther-Jensen, T. 2000a. "Special Issue (23): Notes and Comments, Nigel Grant Festschrift." *Comparative Education* 36 (2): 127–128.

Winther-Jensen, T., ed. 2000b. "Special Issue (23) *Nigel Grant* Festschrift." *Comparative Education* 36 (2).

Hechtius (1795–1798) – the beginnings of historical-philosophical-idiographic research in comparative education

Volker Lenhart

ABSTRACT
From its very beginnings, we can discern two methodological approaches to comparative education; one broadly historical-philosophical-idiographic and another broadly empirical-positivist-nomothetic. Friedrich August Hecht's 1795–1798 *De re scholastica Anglica cum Germanica comparata* (*English and German school education compared*), with its hermeneutic textbook analysis, represents an idiographic methodology. Whilst the 1816/1817 data-driven research programme of Marc-Antoine Jullien – usually considered the origin of comparative education – represents an empirical-positivist-nomothetic approach. In this essay, we will examine the theoretical orientations of Hecht's study – his ideas of transnationality and national character, and his avoidance of the proposal of borrowing and lending. We situate the beginnings of Hecht's methodology in its social-historical context and analyse the transfer of interpretation methods from philology to comparative education. Finally, we will postulate a combination of Jullien's and Hecht's methodological approaches.

Two methodological approaches at the beginning of comparative education

The historical narrative of comparative education usually starts with the research programme of French revolutionary, military officer, journalist, and writer Marc-Antoine Jullien (Fraser 1964). However, about 20 years earlier, a Saxon grammar school principal, Friedrich August Hecht, presented an inquiry into school education in two different national settings. *De re scholastica Anglica cum Germanica comparata* – or *English and German school education compared* (1795–1798; reedited by Lenhart 2015). Thus, the two founding fathers developed the two methodological approaches that can be traced through the history of the discipline: an interpretive historical-philosophical-idiographic approach (Hecht) and a data generating empirical-positivist-nomothetic one (Jullien). And whilst Jullien's position has been spelled out in several commentaries,[1] the approach of Hecht has yet to be explained. To better contextualise Hecht's methodological procedure we need to look at his professional origin, self-ascribed status and the reception of his work, as well as an overview of his study.

Professional origin and self-ascribed status

Hecht was the principal of Freiberg's grammar school. Freiberg was a mining city on the cusp of industrialisation and its citizens looked to industrial England as a model for innovation. In this Hecht was no different; he used school programs – printed invitations to events like year-end assemblies and memorial ceremonies – to share his study and display to the public his knowledge of European school developments. Hecht believed that he was the first to compare 'the education conditions of the individual peoples of our time' (Hechtius reedited by Lenhart 2015, 121) and compared this to an earlier account of schooling within one nation (Ruhkopf 1794). In so doing, he gave the later disciplines of history of education and comparative education the same starting point. Finding studies across historical periods and between nations 'certainly beneficial' (Hechtius reedited by Lenhart 2015, 121), he invited others to do the same.

Reception

Though seldom mentioned in historiographies of comparative education, Hecht's text was never totally forgotten. After acknowledgments in the nineteenth century, for example, by Niemeyer in 1829, he began to be mentioned once more around 1960. Hermann Ody (1959, 66), historian and comparativist of education, used Hecht's study in his book on the educational encounters between England, France and Germany from the beginning of the nineteenth century. American comparativist William Brickman (1960, 7) probably came across the part of the text that is preserved in the New York Public Library when he wrote:

> Another type of eighteenth century study of comparative education … was … by Hecht. Published in 1795 at Freiburg [sic] this Latin work examined comparatively the schools of England and Germany. For the most part it was a descriptive analysis, but the author made some efforts of comparison.

Through Ody, Hecht reappeared in the works of German comparativists (e.g. Hilker 1962; Hartmann 2009). He is also mentioned in French (Giraud 1975), Spanish (Rodriguez 2008) and Polish (Kuba and Pekowska 2011) texts, but it is probable that none of the authors since Ody and Brickman had actually read Hecht directly. Brickman's mention of Hecht received little attention in Britain, despite the fact that the essay is preserved in the Scottish National Library in Edinburgh (Lenhart 2016).

Overview of Hecht's study

The central approach of the treatise is a comparative analysis of English and German textbooks used in English public schools and German Latin and Grammar Schools. Hechtius – the Latin styling of Hecht – focuses on Latin and Greek grammar books, dictionaries, and excerpts from and commented editions of antique Roman and Greek authors. He also analyses textbooks for the subjects of religion, geography and history.

In the late 1770s, King George III of England sent about 80 textbooks from the royal schools of Westminster and Eton to the Göttingen philologist Christian Gottlob Heyne (1729–1812). Heyne was to review the books and find which of them could be used to improve the quality of teaching and learning in the Latin schools of Hannover. In

1780, Heyne published an article on the books, and it was this that gave Hecht the opportunity to compare them to the books available in his school library. Hecht also gathered information on the characteristics of school organisation, curricula and teaching methodology of English public schools from the reports of German travellers (Wendeborn 1785; Küttner 1791–1796). He interpreted these accounts from the perspective of his own experiences in urban German grammar schools; he himself had evidently never been to England. The focus on the public schools explains why Hecht does not include schoolbooks for mathematics and the natural sciences in his comparison. The public schools of his time had a purely classical curriculum; the sciences were taught only privately.

In his study, Hecht underlines the spirit of competition in English public schools as a stimulus for the continuous work of the students. 'The English left no stone unturned in their attempts to stir up competition and thus excite the spirit of young people' (Hechtius ed. Lenhart 2015, 148). As well as awards to honour the best performers, Hecht was impressed by the English implementation of discipline:

> The students at these schools, ranging in age from about 8 to 18, were all held to the same level of discipline … The school's head teacher holds most power over the school. He exercises a certain jurisdiction over everything in the school building and anything regarding the students. The difference between German and English rectors is quite evident. German rectors are not only responsible for individual speeches and facts, which they must abide by as a result of old rules, but also take the blame from parents for ill-administered discipline. (Hechtius ed. Lenhart 2015, 150–151)

Though Hecht had studied at Leipzig University under the tutorship of Ernesti, a leading representative of the German philological neo-humanism, he is not influenced by the philosophical-idealist neo-humanism of, for example, Wilhelm von Humboldt that formed in the nineteenth century the classical curriculum of the German academic preparatory school.

Hecht had not yet elaborated a theory of comparison, but he does go over commonalities and differences. He explains the common traits of the English public and the German grammar schools by the European humanist tradition. He finds differences in teaching methods:

> When it comes to methods of learning and teaching, the English and the Germans are markedly different in terms of praxis and meaning. In particular the English believe that significant progress in literary science is dependent on the young student's fluency in terms of learning, preparing, reading, and practicing and therefore have fewer classes. They nearly laugh at the Germans, whose boys and adolescents attend classes to the point of nausea and spend the rest of the day playing games and engaging in recreational activities. (Hechtius ed. Lenhart 2015, 147)

In Hecht's argumentation, there is a certain tension between two concepts (for which the terms did not yet exist): transnationality of education and national character in education.

With respect to transnationality, Hecht saw education from three perspectives: the influence of transnational royal families on educational policies; the importance of Latin as the common transnational European medium of communication amongst learned humanists and scientists; and the persistence of the tradition of the European classical-humanist curriculum.

Meanwhile, his concept of the national character contained four elements:

(1) A result of the merging of school education and societal socialisation, with emphasis on the latter. Liberal societal socialisation, with freedom of speech at its core, provides an important trait of English national attitudes:

> When it comes to expressing their opinions, the English follow their own judgment and do not look to others with authority. Therefore, the young are praised when they do the same and do not rely on someone else's authority … This freedom of judgment is limited by rules and punishments in schools and academies … . This is why they value the youth's freedom of opinion so highly. They want them to be able to fearlessly represent their views to all without regard for dignity, and to balk at no one's authority, continuing to do so as they grow older. Authorities carry less weight with the English, and what matters to them is not who says something, but rather what they say. No one is so old or worthy that he can inherently derive authority from it. One is thought of as a foolish blatherer if he does not assert himself with the weight of his argument. Neither wrinkles nor riches free him from this responsibility. Common sense, as they call it, is viewed as the highest mental virtue and preferred by every doctrine. It is said that this attitude accounts for the large number of people in this nation who use good judgment about affairs in their public and private lives. (Hechtius ed. Lenhart 2015, 157)

(2) It is modelled according to educated individuals, and so to middle and upper social groups within a society (without focusing solely on dominant elites).
(3) It has no offensive connotations (as often in twentieth-century research when the idea was used to state the negative characteristics of a hostile nation).
(4) It signifies an unavoidable fateful hardship (like the 'iron cage' of Max Weber or the 'societal character' of Erich Fromm):

> If a youth who was born in England grows up in a foreign land and remains there until around his 16th birthday so that he becomes accustomed to the ruling customs of the country, he will not be found fit for any jobs after his return to the fatherland. He will live among his countrymen like a foreigner, thinking he is disdained by all. His own country of birth and fatherland will not recognise him as a citizen. The same fate awaits a German accustomed to English ways since childhood who is then brought back home. (Hechtius ed. Lenhart 2015, 157)

For comparative purposes, it is interesting to note how Hecht tries to resolve the tension between transnationality and national character. He thought the transnational elements of formal schooling limited the extent to which national character could form; and that national character was shaped by societal forces such as non-formal and informal educational processes. Thus, within a given cultural setting, like that of Europe since antiquity, schools provide similarities (transnationality), whilst informal education may produce differences in national character.

Early modern Europe had nations and states, but not nation-states. Hecht had no explicit definition of a nation. The contexts in which he uses the term show that he thinks of a nation as a unit formed by common history, tradition and language. The frequent references to 'fathers' and 'parents' also bring descent (without any biologistic bias) into the concept. As for the state, he mentions the political functions of state order and state action. If nation and state are congruent, then a nation-state exists. For Hecht, the Germans are a nation in the ancient sense of the word, whereas the English are – or are becoming – a state-based nation, and Great Britain is a nation-state.

Thus, comparative education starts with Hecht's essay in a period when the old trans-national order of nations and states was being transformed into the new international order of nation-states (cf. Lenhart 2015, 35–37, 2016, 225).[2]

Hecht does not focus on international 'borrowing and lending' in education. So, with the exception of creating competition in schools, England is not a reference society to be followed, and neither is Germany – as some international observers in the nineteenth century proposed.

Details of Hecht's methodological position

In contrast to Jullien, Hecht relies more on data interpretation than on data collection. He interprets two kinds of data: printed texts and his own professional experiences. He considers textbooks as an important source. For England, he has reports of German travellers. For Germany too he has written references but relies mainly on his own views and his experiences in Saxony.

To understand details of Hecht's methodological position, it is useful to look at an essay that he published some years after his comparative treatise. In 1809, as a philologist interpreting classical Greek and Roman authors, he published *De variis interpretandi generibus eorumque recto usu* (*On the different genres of interpretation and their correct use*). In the first sentence of the essay, he writes clearly about the relationship between his philological considerations and pedagogical issues: 'A big part of the task to be fulfilled in school by the teachers of the upper grades is that of interpreting correctly Greek and Roman authors. For this, no special proof is needed' (Hechtius 1809, 2).

Interpretation is for him not mere translation, but understanding by covering the full meaning of written information. Thus, he enumerates the following 'genres of interpretation':

- the *grammatical* approach: the reader must have a full knowledge of the grammatical structure of a phrase;
- the *lexical* perspective: the genealogy of individual words has to be understood;
- the *philosophical* mode: for example, in a sentence dealing with juvenile morality it has to be clarified what virtue is, what evil is, what it means to be an adolescent, what human greatness is;
- the *rhetorical* type: it has to be found out which opinions or attitudes the author wants to provoke in the reader;
- the *historical* way: the historical setting in which a statement was formulated has to be understood;
- the *aesthetic* mode: especially in poetic texts, the beauty of the wording has to be remarked and
- the *critical* kind: it has to be proven that the version of the text is really the authentic and original one and which conjectures have to be made.

Methods transfer from philology to comparative education

Which of the above remarks of the classical philologist are applied in Hecht's work?

In his textbook analysis, all approaches can be found. Grammars and lexica are important school media themselves[3] (Hechtius ed. Lenhart 2015, 127–134 for teaching Latin, 139–141 for learning Greek). When dealing with editions of ancient orators or the inherent tendencies of (not only ancient) writers the rhetorical mode is used:

> Some prefer using texts by newer authors that were published specifically for beginning Latin instruction. These texts cover more contemporary subjects, which has the advantage of saving time as teachers are not obliged to explain the customs or conditions of antiquity. Furthermore, stories about nature or morals nearer to our time offer more appeal than those from long ago. One can see this in the works of Erasmus. He is critical of works that do not appropriately match topics to the spirit of youth, denouncing them as ignorant. (Hechtius ed. Lenhart 2015, 135)

When talking about the art of construction of the Greek comedy, or the elegance of Cicero's and Caesar's prose, an aesthetic element appears in the didactical reflection: 'Among those qualified to judge none can deny the charms in Caesar's simplicity and that his manner of speaking is a treasure of oration' (Hechtius ed. Lenhart 2015, 137). The critical approach is not only used to prove whether editions of classical texts are valid, but also whether the content of a textbook is true. In detailing the approach Hecht develops two pedagogical subcategories. First, is the correct content structured in a way that enables learning? Second, is the presentation adequate to the cognitive level of the students?

Sometimes the historical and philosophical types of interpretation occur in the textbook analysis, for example, when warnings are issued on lascivious passages in ancient texts, but their main field of utilisation goes beyond textbook inspection purposes. When Hecht reflects on the history of teaching Latin in Germany, the historical approach is obvious (Hechtius ed. Lenhart 2015, 129). When he elucidates the basic orientation of English education ideas, he uses the philosophical lens:

> The English, unlike the Germans, do not seek out fundamental guidance and practices on the raising of children from books. They (for example) do not value the reading of nor do they turn to the valuable and well-known work of Locke for guidelines in raising their youth ... This does not mean, however, that the English leave everything to chance. It would seem that human nature serves as their guide – within the constraints of their model of societal organisation ... It is fixed in the English consciousness that every man is distinguished with intellect and will be guided to a way of life suitable for him by a natural drive ... Those who resist nature do so in vain. Parents are reprimanded if they push their children towards a particular lifestyle for which they do not have the resources of nature. This leads to the conviction that youth should be allowed freedom from an early age in order to prevent their developing servile attitudes, hiding mistakes from their fathers and teachers and thereby avoiding every inconvenient path. One cannot deny that the English often overshoot their target. They are far too lenient with corrupt behavior, an indulgence that often leads to the corruption and ruin of adult sons. Since the English generally are very focused on the freedom of citizens, they want to share this advantage with their children. They believe if young men are offered the sweetness of freedom, they will go on to become the strongest preservers and defenders of it for the remainder of their lives. They do not find freedom of judgment a risk, but rather provide ample opportunity for practice. (Hechtius ed. Lenhart 2015, 155)

With the application of his philological interpretation to aspects of his comparative essay, he introduces into the discipline the methodological orientation that was later systematised in German epistemology by Dilthey (1961, 1968), as an operation called 'Verstehen'.[4] The nineteenth-century philosopher saw 'Verstehen' (deep understanding) as appropriate in the humanities whilst the natural sciences use 'Erklären' (causal explaining) for their findings.

Conclusions

In his epilogue to the 2015 re-edition of Hecht's essay, Phillips (2015, 161–163) sketches the advantages of Hecht's work:

- It is 'a brave attempt' to compare the curriculum and its implementation in the countries in reference. Today such an effort would be made 'in terms what is prescribed or normal or expected'.
- Hecht uses his information 'to exemplify some aspects of the wider function of schools that throw practice in the two countries into interesting context'.
- The Saxon principal 'shows a refreshing humour in his depiction of English schooling'. Hecht is not an ivory tower idealist but a man who knows the reality of school education.

Phillips also identifies the main weaknesses of Hecht's text as seen from a contemporary perspective. First, the 'units of comparison are problematic'. This refers to the public schools that were taken as representative for English grammar schools. They were outstanding and it is not clear whether in Germany there were schools of that status. Another problem is the reference unit of Germany before it became 'Prussian' Germany 1871. Second, the characteristics Hecht ascribes to schools at least for the English side are not entirely based on evidence. Third, the detailed analyses of school books do not substitute a description of types of schools that are about to form an education system. Lastly, by avoiding 'borrowing and lending' Hecht does not try to draw lessons from his comparison.

The achievements illustrate what can be reached with Hecht's methodology. But the deficiencies, especially the lack of empirical data collection, mark the limits of the approach. To develop, Hecht's methodological paradigm needs a method of data generation other than a review of the literature and their interpretation – for example, qualitative content analysis. From Jullien's side, it needs an improvement in the methods of data collection, like the refinement of the interviews and observations he pursued in Pestalozzi's school, and a precision of statistical analysis of his quantitative findings.

Epstein (2017, 328) is right when he states that the quality of both authors' work (those of Jullien and Hecht) must be judged according to the possibilities of their time, and not by research standards developed two centuries later. For a thorough understanding of education in different societal and national contexts both approaches must be combined (mixed methods, cf. Creswell 2015). This includes methodological design *and* topic-oriented theoretical framework (for example, the different functions of comparative analysis).[5] Today in comparative studies the mixed-methods approach is the mainstream, though in any single approach a preponderance of either idiographic or nomothetic methodology may be visible.

Notes

1. Fraser (1964); Giraud (1975); Gautherin (1993); and Adick (2008, 22) who says:

Jullien's model was the natural sciences. His approach was empirical, he intended to collect facts and observations, to put these together in tables, out of which mathematical calculations could be drawn that lead to rules and laws for better teaching and learning. For that purpose he developed a questionnaire with not less than 266 questions.

2. To continue speculation on Hecht's lines one may say that the more states became nation-states, the more national character invaded (Ushinsky 1857/1975) or at least also shaped (Sadler, cf. Phillips 2006) school education. With today's supra-nationalism as in the EU or glo-balisation, the tendency of development is inverted again.
3. Examples include: *A short introduction to grammar for the use of lower forms in the King's School at Westminster* (London 1776); *Busbian Grammar, Extended and Revised. Metrical Foundations of Greek and Latin Grammar* (London 1778) (noted by Hecht without more bibliographic details).
4. Cf. Abel (1948): the operation called 'Verstehen'. *American Journal of Sociology* 54, 211–218.
5. Epstein (2008) calls this the middle position of 'historical functionalism' which he links to authors like Kazamias and Massialas (1982), Gerbert (1993) or to his own publication of 2006. To follow Epstein's perspective in German comparative literature a look at the publications of Röhrs (e.g. 1995, 63–65 'hermeneutic-empirical method') or the more recent textbook of Waterkamp (2006) or the edition by Parreira do Amaral and Amos (2015) is illustrative.

Acknowledgements

With permission of the copyright holders, some parts of the 'summary of the introduction' of the author's edition (2015) and the author's article (2016) were re-used for this text.

Disclosure statement

No potential conflict of interest was reported by the author.

References

Abel, T. J. G. 1948. "The Operation Called 'Verstehen'." *American Journal of Sociology* 54: 211–218.
Adick, Ch. 2008. *Vergleichende Erziehungswissenschaft. Eine Einführung*. Stuttgart: Kohlhammer.
Brickman, W. 1960. "A Historical Introduction to Comparative Education." *Comparative Education Review* 3 (3): 6–13.
Creswell, J. W. 2015. *A Concise Introduction to Mixed Methods Research*. Los Angeles, CA: Sage.
Dilthey, W. 1961. *Pädagogik – Geschichte und System*. 3rd ed. Gottingen: Vandenhoek und Ruprecht.
Dilthey, W. 1968. *Die geistige Welt, 1. Abhandlungen zur Grundlegung der Geisteswissenschaften*. 5th ed. Gottingen: Vandenhoek und Ruprecht.
Epstein, E. H. 2008. "Setting the Normative Boundaries: Crucial Epistemological Benchmarks in Comparative Education." *Comparative Education* 44 (4): 373–386.
Epstein, E. H. 2017. "Is Marc-Antoine Jullien de Paris the 'Father' of Comparative Education?" *Compare: A Journal of Comparative and International Education* 47 (3): 317–331.
Fraser, S. 1964. *Jullien's Plan for Comparative Education 1816–1817*. New York: Teachers College Columbia University.
Gautherin, J. 1993. "Marc-Antoine Jullien de Paris (1775–1848)." *Perspectives. Revue trimestrielle d' éducation compare* 23: 783–798.

Gerbert, E. 1993. "Lessons from the 'Kokugo' (National Language) Readers." *Comparative Education Review* 37 (2): 152–180.

Giraud, J. 1975. "Marc-Antoine Jullien de Paris (1775–1848)." *Paedagogica Historica: International Journal of the History of Education* 15: 379–405.

Hartmann, B. 2009. *Die Anfänge der Vergleichenden Erziehungswissenschaft im deutschsprachigen Raum. Das Wirken des Erziehungswissenschaftlers Friedrich Schneider.* Frankfurt a.M.: Lang.

Hechtius, F. A. 1795–1798. *De re scholastica Anglica cum Germanica comparata.* Freiberg: Gerlach.

Hechtius, F. A. 1809. *De variis interpretandi generibus eorumque recto usu.* Freiberg: Gerlach.

Hilker, F. 1962. *Vergleichende Pädagogik.* München: Hueber.

Kazamias, A., and B. G. Massialas. 1982. *Comparative Education. An Encyclopedia of Educational Research.* 5th ed. Edited by H. E. Mitzel, 309–317. New York: Free Press.

Kuba, E., and K. Pekowska. 2011. "Pedagogika Porownawca." Accessed October 2017. http://www.docpöayer.pl/2225049-Pedagogica Porownawcza.

Küttner, G. 1791–1796. *Beiträge zur Kenntnis vorzüglich des Innern von England und seiner Einwohner. Aus Briefen eines Freundes gezogen von dem Herausgeber.* Leipzig: Dyk.

Lenhart, V. Hrsg, ed. 2015. *Die erste Schrift zur Vergleichenden Erziehungswissenschaft. The First Treatise in Comparative Education. Fridericus Augustus Hechtius: De re scholastica Anglica cum Germanica comparata (1795–1798).* Lateinisches Original, deutsche und englische Übersetzung/Latin Original, German and English Translation. Nachwort von David Phillips/Epilogue by David Phillips. Frankfurt: Peter Lang.

Lenhart, V. 2016. "The First Treatise in Comparative Education Rediscovered." *Research in Comparative and International Education* (SAGE Journals) 11: 222–226.

Niemeyer, A. H. 1829. *Grundsätze der Erziehung und des Unterrichts für Aeltern, Hauslehrer und Schulmänner. Dritter Band.* Wien: Meusberger.

Ody, H. J. 1959. *Begegnung zwischen Deutschland, England und Frankreich im höheren Schulwesen seit Beginn des 19. Jahrhunderts.* Saarbrücken: Gesellschaft für bildendes Schrifttum.

Parreira do Amaral, M., and S. K. Amos. 2015. "Internationale und Vergleichende Erziehungswissenschaft. Geschichte, Theorie, Methode und Forschungsfelder." *New Frontiers in Comparative Education 2.* Muenster: Waxmann.

Phillips, D. 2006. "Michael Sadler and Comparative Education." *Oxford Review of Education* 32 (1): 39–54.

Phillips, D. 2015. "Nachwort/Epilogue." In *Die erste Schrift zur Vergleichenden Erziehungswissenschaft/ The first Treatise in Comparative Education. Fridericus Augustus Hechtius: De re scholastica Anglica cum Germanica comparata (1795–1798),* edited by V. Lenhart, Hrsg. Lateinisches Original, deutsche und englische Übersetzung/Latin Original, German and English Translation, 161–163. Frankfurt: Peter Lang.

Rodriguez, A. 2008. "La educación comparada durante el siglo XIX." *Aportaciones Alemanas.* Accessed November 2014. de.Slideshare.net/arlinesrodriguez/gnesis-de-la-educacion-comparada?related=1.

Röhrs, H. 1995. *Die Vergleichende und Internationale Erziehungswissenschaft. Gesammelte Schriften Bd.3.* Weinheim: Deutscher Studienverlag.

Ruhkopf, F. E. 1794. *Geschichte des Schul- und Erziehungswesens in Deutschland, von der Einführung des Christenthums bis auf die neuesten Zeiten, Erster Theil.* Bremen: Wilman.

Ushinsky, K. D. (1857) 1975. "On National Character of Public Education." In *Selected Works,* edited by A. J. Piskunov, 100–207. Moscow: Progress Publishers.

Waterkamp, D. 2006. *Vergleichende Erziehungswissenschaft. Ein Lehrbuch.* Münster: Waxmann.

Wendeborn, G. F. A. 1785. *Der Zustand des Staats, der Religion, der Gelehrsamkeit und Kunst in Großbritannien gegen Ende des achtzehnten Jahrhunderts.* Berlin: Spener.

Bereday and Hilker: origins of the 'four steps of comparison' model

Christel Adick

ABSTRACT

The article draws attention to the forgotten ancestry of the *four steps of comparison* model (description – interpretation – juxtaposition – comparison). Comparativists largely attribute this to George Z. F. Bereday [1964. *Comparative Method in Education*. New York: Holt, Rinehart and Winston], but among German scholars, it is mostly attributed to Franz Hilker [1962. *Vergleichende Pädagogik*. München: Max Hueber]. Who, then, is the rightful author of the model? This article attempts to answer this question. The methodological approaches of the two authors will be compared and contextualised in respect to their academic lives, especially through the 1950s and 1960s. Hilker and Bereday both referred to each other's publications on several occasions, which indicates a close communication between them. In contrast to the Anglophone dominance of scientific journals today, their way of practising comparative education was multilingual. Their cooperation with the nascent national academic associations of those times is also examined. Finally, the epistemological characteristics of the *four steps* model, including its limitations, and value for the field of comparative education today, are evaluated.

Introduction

This paper aims to reveal the origins of the *four steps of comparison* model (description – interpretation – juxtaposition – comparison) attributed either to George Z. F. Bereday (1964) or to Franz Hilker (1962). The answer seems to be that both may be called the progenitors of this model. Hilker seems to have been the first to canonise the four steps and to have given them their final terminology: description, interpretation, juxtaposition and comparison. This was evidently approved and taken up by Bereday, who in turn authored the visual model widely familiar from the international literature. Over time, Hilker's contribution to the model seems to have been forgotten in the scientific community, possibly because his publications were written in German. He has disappeared from references in the international (Anglophone) literature, but – what is even more vexing – his part in the origin of the four steps of comparison is no longer mentioned even in recent German literature.

The (alleged) authorship of the *four steps of comparison* model: a brief survey of the literature

Maria Manzon (2007, 86–87) clearly attributes the *four steps of comparison* model to Bereday. She distinguishes between two main 'purposes of comparison' – interpretive or causal-analytic – and classifies Bereday's approach as interpretive. Her text includes Bereday's graphic model (cf. Figure 1) and highlights the fact that, according to Bereday, 'the purpose of juxtaposition […] was to establish a *tertium comparationis*, "the criterion upon which a valid comparison can be made and the hypothesis for which it is

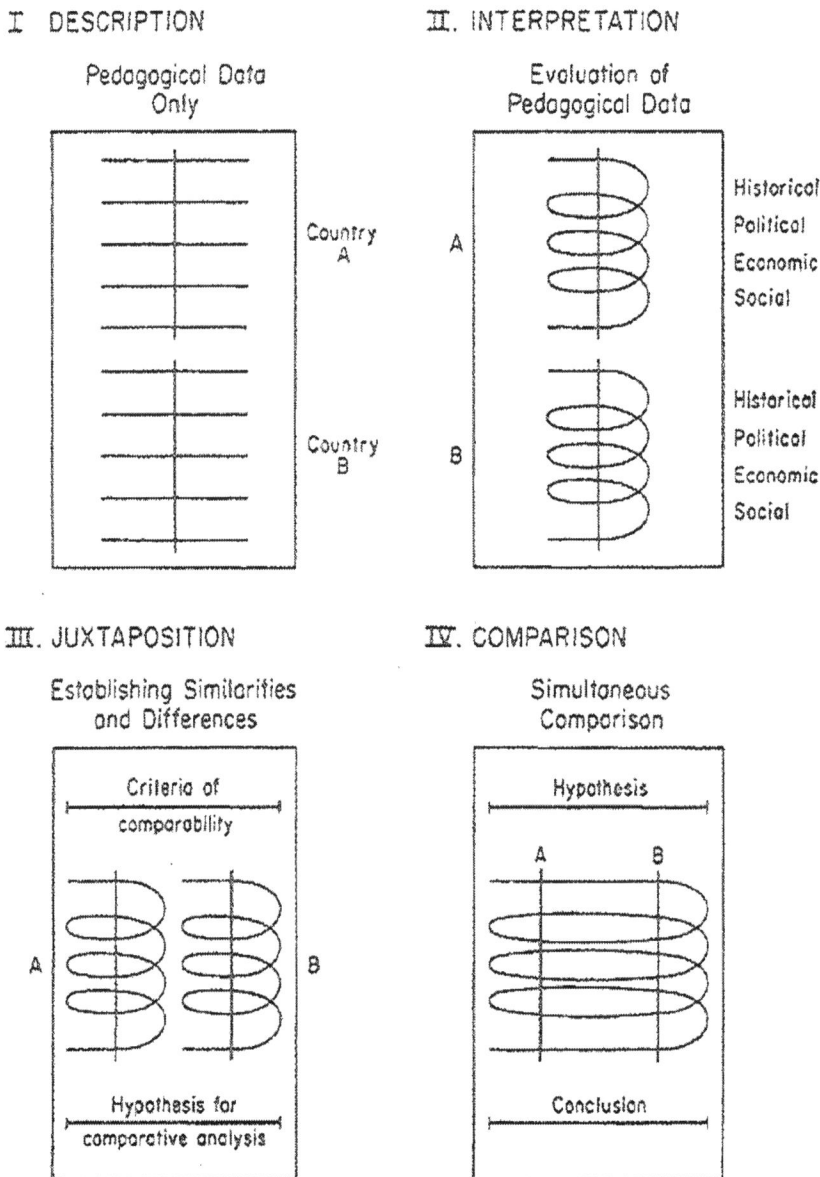

I. DESCRIPTION — Pedagogical Data Only — Country A — Country B

II. INTERPRETATION — Evaluation of Pedagogical Data — Historical, Political, Economic, Social (A) — Historical, Political, Economic, Social (B)

III. JUXTAPOSITION — Establishing Similarities and Differences — Criteria of comparability — Hypothesis for comparative analysis — A — B

IV. COMPARISON — Simultaneous Comparison — Hypothesis — A — B — Conclusion

Figure 1. Bereday's model for undertaking comparative studies. Source: Bereday (1964, 28).

to be made"'. By contrast, I myself have discussed the four steps of comparison as Hilker's invention, referencing his book on comparative pedagogy[1] (1962, 106–126). I paraphrase Hilker's four steps, discuss the methodological limitations of the model, and highlight Hilker's concern for a *tertium comparationis* (Adick 2008, 144–147).

The point is that I do not reference Bereday, and Manzon does not mention Hilker. This is despite the fact that the missing works are both comprehensive books and not merely articles which one might have overlooked. This might suggest that the model is claimed according to language-group: Hilker in the German and Bereday in Anglophone literature. With English as the predominant language in the wider international scientific community, Bereday has become known as the originator of the model while Hilker's contribution has been forgotten.

As might be expected, Bereday's model is cited in publications on comparative education published in English (e.g. Bray 2004; Phillips and Schweisfurth 2014). Meanwhile, Hilker appears as the author of the model in German publications. In Stübig's (1997) comparison of the relevance of Friedrich Schneider and Franz Hilker for comparative education in post-war Germany, he summarises Hilker's four steps without mentioning Bereday. The same occurs in follow-up research conducted under the auspices of DIPF (i.e. *The German Institute for International Educational Research*) on the first Programme for International Student Assessment (PISA) findings in Germany. The authors[2] explicitly refer to Hilker's model as their guiding principle (Arbeitsgruppe Internationale Vergleichsstudie 2003, 28). Yet Bereday is named as the author of the four steps model sometimes even in German language publications. For example, in his book on comparative education, Waterkamp (2006, 202–203) reports in detail on the methods and findings of Rothe (2001) who had studied professional education systems of Germany, Austria and Switzerland by explicitly claiming to follow Bereday's model, without mentioning Hilker. Likewise, Parreira do Amaral (2015) introduces the model as 'the comparative method according to Bereday' (114–117), mentioning only later in the text and in brackets only 'cf. Hilker 1962' (115), which seemingly suggests an attribution of the authorship of the *four steps of comparison* model to Bereday.

These examples suggest that most comparativists are unaware of the problems in their referencing only Bereday (or less often only Hilker) as the originator of the model. One exception is Jose Luis García Garrido, who attributes the model to both Bereday and Hilker in his introductory textbook (Garrido and Luis 1996, 148). Taking up this challenge,[3] I began to look into the origins of the model in an article aimed at a German audience (Adick 2014a). The present contribution will build on this by including more information on the academic context of the *four steps of comparison* model, as well as biographical notes on Bereday and Hilker.

Hilker *or* Bereday? Hilker *and* Bereday?

Before reconstructing the origins of the *four steps of comparison* model, it should be understood that Hilker and Bereday knew each other. They seemed to have respected each other, read each other's works, and quoted and referenced each other on several occasions. This suggests that their relationship was cooperative rather than competitive or adversarial.[4] With this in mind, it is surprising to discover that in his exploration of the four steps, Hilker (1962, 107–126) does not mention any previous works or contribution by Bereday in formulating his model, even though Bereday is referenced in the text. Similarly, in Bereday's book (1964), the terminology *description – interpretation – juxtaposition and comparison* (the last two points are discussed together and not separately) is applied without any reference to Hilker (1962). Why is this? Bereday's book was published two years after Hilker's; it should be expected that he would have at least mentioned Hilker when discussing the model. Why didn't he? We will try to find out by looking into Bereday's book, as well as examining earlier publications for clues that might solve the puzzle.

Bereday (1964) begins his book by discussing the *raison d'être* of comparative education. He includes short reviews of the methodological contributions of historical figures in the discipline such as Marc-Antoine Jullien, Leo Tolstoy, Michael Sadler, Isaac Kandel, including the German authors Friedrich Schneider and Franz Hilker (1964, 7). He then discusses the 'area studies' approach under which he includes country studies. In a sub-chapter, he explicitly highlights first the challenges of *description* (1964, 11ff.) and then of *interpretation* (18ff.). In another sub-chapter on 'comparative studies' (21ff.), he jointly discusses *juxtaposition and comparison* (22f.) by presenting the *problem approach* of Brian Holmes (23ff. and footnote 24, page 269) and so-called *total analysis* (25ff.), which he defines like this:

> Only after working on countless problems and doggedly accumulating experience in research should comparative educators turn to total analysis. The concern with the over-all impact of education upon society in a world perspective is the culminating point of the discipline. [...]. As in all social sciences, this final stage of the discipline is concerned with the formulation of 'laws' or 'typologies' that permit an international understanding and a definition of the complex interrelation between the schools and the people they serve. The total analysis, as the term indicates, deals with the immanent general forces upon which all systems are built. (ibid. 25)

From the structure of this chapter, we can say that, according to Bereday, *description and interpretation* are strongly connected with the idiographic type of area or country study. Meanwhile, *juxtaposition and comparison* are directed to focus on well-defined research questions (like the *problem approach*) or to extract and arrive at generalisations (laws, typologies as in the *total analysis*). Only at the end of this chapter does Bereday explicitly integrate both sets of arguments into:

> First description, the systematic collection of pedagogical information in one country, then interpretation, the analysis in terms of social sciences, then juxtaposition, a simultaneous review of several systems to determine the framework in which to compare them, and finally comparison, first of select problems and then of the total relevance of education in several countries – these four steps (Fig. 3) point the way to the future for comparative education. (Bereday 1964, 27–28)

'Fig. 3' is his famous graphic illustration of the four steps (cf. Figure 1) which has often been reproduced in the literature (for example, in Manzon 2007, 86; Adick 2014a, 21; Parreira do Amaral 2015, 116 and elsewhere).

It should be remarked that the characteristic labelling of the four steps as they are known in academic discourse (*description – interpretation – juxtaposition – comparison*) do not stand out in Bereday's text in any way (e.g. as subtitles); only at the end of the elaboration are they epitomised as the headings of the four parts of the illustration (cf. Figure 1). We can note also that neither Bereday's summary of the four steps (quoted above) nor his illustration (reproduced above) contain any mention of Hilker. However, a closer look at the footnotes of the chapter throws some light on the context in which the ideas originated. Bereday writes in his first footnote that he had already presented an earlier version of this chapter on several occasions and in different languages: in 1960 at the Sorbonne, Paris (French); in 1961 in Moscow (Russian), and in 1962 in Tokyo (English). Bereday then hints at a version which had been published in German for the *Festschrift* for Friedrich Schneider edited by Wolfgang Brezinka. He adds that he had already presented the contents of this chapter in lectures at different universities. From this footnote, it can be concluded that Bereday had produced some oral or written versions of his model since 1960, in any case before he incorporated them into his book. Would a written manuscript of his 1960 presentation at the Sorbonne in French still exist? Are any of such previous versions identical with his 1964 book publication? Had any of these lectures reached German scholars including Hilker? From when onwards did Bereday utilise the illustration? All these questions are left for future researchers to solve.

One piece of evidence connects Bereday with German; his contribution to the *Festschrift* devoted to Friedrich Schneider (the other internationally renowned German comparativist) (Bereday 1961a). This article was published prior to Hilker's book, and was known to Hilker who could have quoted it while writing his chapter on the four steps (Hilker 1962). After a short historical review, Bereday's article in the *Festschrift* presents, as he says, his 'own variant of comparative analysis', which consists of 'two steps' titled 'area study' and 'comparative study' (1961a, 145), each of which is then subdivided into two sections: area study contains (a) the 'geography of education' and (b) the 'application of other social sciences'; while comparative study consists of (a) the 'problem approach' and (b) 'total analysis' (145–159). This pattern can be interpreted as a forerunner of the chapter in his book as depicted above. But there is a certain inconsistency in that Bereday speaks of 'two steps' at the beginning of his article, whereas in resuming his argument at the end, he speaks of 'these four steps of processing' which lead comparative pedagogy into the future (159).[5] It is also important to note that throughout the article, there is no mention of the terms *description, interpretation, juxtaposition, comparison* and so at that time Bereday did not (yet) associate these terms with his nascent 2×2, i.e. four steps.

The answer to our question becomes clearer when we consider further Bereday's book (1964) in which he references Hilker in respect of the four steps, if only in the second chapter (i.e. *after* he has presented the model in the first chapter). This second chapter compares school reforms in France and in Turkey by applying the concept of comparison. Its first extensive footnote is important in that it reads:

> An earlier version of this chapter was read as a working paper at the second annual eastern regional conference of the Comparative Education Society on April 29, 1960 at Teachers College, Columbia University. It was published in German in *Bildung und Erziehung* as 'Schulreformen in Frankreich und der Türkei – Versuch einer systematischen Vergleichung', Vol. 14, Heft 4 (April 1961), pp. 246–258. The four steps of classification of procedure first proposed in that article were later happily named by Franz Hilker in *Vergleichende Pädagogik* (München: Hueber, 1962) as description, interpretation, juxtaposition, and comparison. That terminology (in part derived from other writers in the field, such as Pedro Rosselló) has been adopted throughout this book. (ibid. footnote 1, 270)

This means that in his earlier publications, Bereday (1961a, 1961b) operated with 'four steps', but without the terminology as we know it – which came from Hilker's book, in which Hilker himself attributed the term 'juxtaposition' explicitly to Rosselló (Hilker 1962, 121). Bereday sanctions the concept and adopts the terminology by applying it throughout his 1964 book. At the end of his treatise comparing school reforms in France and Turkey, he resumes his acknowledgement of Hilker's work:

> If instead of off-the-cuff comparisons, students of comparative education forced themselves first to tabulate pedagogical data for each country, then to interpret the data in the light of other social sciences, then to set them side by side to determine their comparability, and finally directly to compare them, they would reach, what Franz Hilker urges as the ideal, 'a clarity of personal grasp and an elevation from subjective understanding to objective precision'. (Bereday 1964, 51)

The adjacent footnote in his book (Bereday 1964, footnote 12, 271) refers to an earlier article by Hilker (1957, 618). This hints that the origin of the concept dates back much further than would be expected if one only reads both authors' books from the 1960s.

It must be stressed that Hilker also referenced Bereday's (1961b) German article on school reforms in France and Turkey while describing his own model. He credits Bereday when utilising 'a steps model'. He then paraphrases the headings that Bereday used which, however, were not yet identical to those Hilker (1962) established in his book and as we know them today: *description – interpretation – juxtaposition – comparison*.

This leads to the question: where did Hilker get these categories? In Hilker's 1957 article (referenced in Bereday's 1964 book), Hilker posits that to compare would involve 'different steps', and he begins with an elaboration of 'the first step' (1957, 614). But then he seems to forget this in what follows: the term 'steps' never appears again, although it is shown (by numbering) that he operates with three points, i.e. 'steps'. There is no mention of a fourth point or 'step' nor of the later terminology – which shows that the concept had not yet been developed in 1957.

As for the question 'Hilker *or/and* Bereday?', we can say that their concepts of the four steps of comparison were *parallel developments*; neither plagiarism nor independent inventions. The concept-building spanned several years, grew out of preceding lectures and articles by each, and entailed mutual references to each other's publications. While *the graphic illustration* of the model is clearly Bereday's contribution, the canonised labelling *description – interpretation – juxtaposition – comparison* stems from Hilker's concept, and was only imported into Bereday's writings when he formulated his graphic model.

Bereday and Hilker: some notes on their biographies and achievements

We will now look at what the two scholars shared in common and at how they differed, and so contextualise what has been discovered about the origins of the *four steps of comparison*.

To begin with the differences, the authors belong to two different generations. Hilker (1881–1969) was born in the nineteenth century and experienced two world wars. Having been dismissed in 1933 from his posts during the Hitler era, he had to re-start his career after the war when he was already approaching retirement. He was in his early 80s when his book on comparative education (Hilker 1962) was published. Bereday (1920–1983) was born after the First World War and had been an active combatant during the Second World War in the Polish and British Armies. His academic career only began after the end of the war. His sudden death at the early age of 63 meant that it lasted less than two decades. When his book on comparative education was published (1964), Bereday was 44 years old. Given the age gap and their different experiences, the fact of such rewarding academic communication between these two academics after the war traversing generations and war alliances should be highlighted.

Hilker had no university career. He had a secondary or high school education (in the German *Gymnasium*), including posts with international affiliations, which he began because of his strong inclination for international comparison and cooperation. Without a doctoral degree, Hilker could not attain a chair at a university; he only became a professor in an academy – the State Arts Academy in Berlin temporarily in the 1930s. He was already in his retirement when, finally, in 1960, he received an honorary doctoral degree from the University of Hamburg. In contrast, Bereday rapidly climbed the US higher education ladder and occupied posts devoted to university-level comparative education. He earned his Ph.D. in sociology and comparative education at Harvard, and taught comparative education at Teachers College, Columbia University (1955–1983).[6] These very different careers, however, did not keep Hilker and Bereday from fruitful academic communication with each other.

Bereday seems to have outperformed any comparativist of the day in this respect. He is said to have been proficient in eight languages.[7] This contrasts sharply with today's quasi-monolingualism in 'global English' as the medium of scientific communication. Hilker was less of a polyglot, although he learnt Latin and Greek as part of his humanistic education and was proficient in English and French. Hilker's education and career were entirely German-focused. Bereday, on the other hand, left Poland and studied and worked in different countries; he attained academic degrees in the UK, then stayed in the USA and held guest professorships in various countries.

So much for these differences. But what did the two men have in common? Hilker and Bereday were both the authors of leading comprehensive introductions to comparative education of the post-war period. Both books are now classics of the discipline, Hilker in German (1962) and Bereday in English (1964). Both authors describe their books as collections based on previous publications. Hilker (1962, 9) writes that his book leans on numerous articles which he had published before (1920–1933) and after (1945–1960) the war. Bereday (1964, vii–xiii) states that several chapters had previously been published, and lists permission to reprint from such publications, beginning with his two articles published in Germany (Bereday 1961a, 1961b). Hilker's and Bereday's seminal books on comparative education may be considered as *the peak of their concept-building* which had grown out of several years of thinking, lecturing and publishing and – not least – of international communication between them and others.

Hilker and Bereday were also among the first and leading personalities in the nascent academic associations in comparative education. The history of the US-based Comparative Education Society (CES) founded in 1956, later renamed the Comparative and International Education Society (CIES) in 1969, is closely connected to Bereday. From there sprang the idea for an international conference in London in May 1961. This led to the founding of the Comparative Education Society in Europe (CESE). The German participants in this – among them Franz Hilker – became the founders of the Comparative Education Commission which, in 1965, was the first to gain the status of an accredited commission of the nascent German Society for Education. Decades later, reorganisation of that German

Society (2000) led to the founding of the Section for International and Intercultural Comparative Education (SIIVE).[8]

Bereday and Hilker were both founders of leading academic journals that still exist today. As early as 1948, Hilker founded *Bildung und Erziehung*, which was and still is very international and comparative even though it does not contain these descriptors in its journal title. In 1957, Bereday became the first editor of the *Comparative Education Review*, the society journal of the US-based CES (later CIES). Each published in the journal of the other, as with Bereday's article (1961b) on school reforms in France and Turkey in *Bildung und Erziehung*, and Hilker's article on what the comparative method can contribute to education in the *Comparative Education Review* (1964). Hilker's death was commemorated in his own German journal in *Bildung und Erziehung*'s first issue of 1969.[9] He was also remembered in English-medium journals: in the *Comparative Education Review* by Brickman (1969), and in *Comparative Education* by Anweiler (1969). Bereday's death was also commemorated in his journal in a special 'in memoriam' issue which contained articles by various authors (*Comparative Education Review* No 1/1984). However, it was not commemorated in the German journal *Bildung und Erziehung*.

Both were internationally minded comparativists. They liked and practised international relations and travelling. In this respect, Hilker's activities in the 1920s before his dismissal in the Nazi era should be noted. As part of his posts at the Zentralinstitut für Erziehung und Unterricht in Berlin, Hilker founded and headed a special Pädagogische Auslandsstelle. He organised fact-finding missions and educational exchanges for foreigners touring in Germany and for Germans visiting abroad (Hilker 1962, 88–90). Such activities involved study tours between the Zentralinstitut and the International Institute of Teachers College, Columbia University, which later became the alma mater of George Bereday (1955) when he became Professor of Comparative Education there. Hilker also published his experiences of such journeys, for example, to the United States (Hilker 1928). Shortly before the Nazis dismissed him, Hilker had begun working for the Commission for Intellectual Cooperation of the League of Nations. After the war, he renewed his international contacts by founding the Pädagogische Arbeitsstelle in Wiesbaden (1947) to continue his prewar tradition of exchange visits. Bereday also took up all the chances of international cooperation and contacts which he encountered in his university career as a professor of comparative education.

Hilker and Bereday were both interested in education in Russia and the Soviet Union. One of Hilker's first publications (1922) treated education in post-revolutionary Russia. According to Anweiler (2013), he had a continued interest in educational developments in Russia and Eastern Europe after the Second World War, which he followed by reading translations in German, English or French of publications by East European authors. Bereday published on Soviet education from the 1960s together with other authors (e.g. Bereday, Brickman, and Read 1960) and extensively in various books and articles, not least because of his guest professorships in Moscow (1960 and 1961). Bereday read publications from the East, because he spoke Polish and Russian.

What is the value of the *four steps of comparison* model today?

Every model has its limitations and the four steps model is no different (cf. Adick 2008, 145–146, 2014b, 231). Firstly, consider the implicit premise of the four steps: How can researchers *describe* let alone *interpret* social reality without any foregoing concepts? For instance, what a school system is, how one conceives of teacher training or how educational success is defined; these should be theorised and defined *before* collecting data and interpreting them. The model is also limited by its inductive methodology:[10] it posits that *juxtaposition* and *comparison* lead to generalisations and hypotheses able to be tested in future research. But epistemologically, conclusions from specificity to generalisations are impossible; a fact well known but often forgotten.[11] Another limitation is the model's implicit methodological nationalism. Hilker and Bereday, like other comparativists, simply assume that the nation-state is the relevant unit of comparison in that national cultural traits can explain educational developments in a given country. This assumption still underpins much comparative research today, but is ever more questioned in the context of globalisation, cross-border migration, and transnational educational biographies and educational organisations across borders.

The model only allows the comparison of a very limited number of cases. As much as it may serve as a valuable blueprint for typical exercises in comparing two countries (or two reforms or two ways of financing schooling, as illustrated in Bereday's graphic model), it becomes impracticable with rising numbers of cases under comparison. The model then appears to be intuitively conclusive for comparisons of a limited number of cases, yet it remains problematic. From an epistemological point of view, the limits of inductive reasoning must be considered. *Description* and *interpretation* might contain implicit assumptions about education in national settings. *Juxtaposition* might turn into a procedure for confronting some over-typified variables in a rather mechanical way. *Comparison* tends to end up in the well-known but often forgotten normative and/or natural fallacies of generalising from *what is* to *what ought to be* (normative fallacy), and/or of concluding from *single cases* to the alleged *universal nature* of something (naturalism, essentialism).

Marc-Antoine Jullien is often described as the founder of comparative education, having been the first to write a treatise (1817) of the new discipline by applying empirical research while emphasising international cooperation (Adick 2008, 15–24). This view is challenged by Lenhart (forthcoming) who discusses the treatise of Friedrich August Hecht, who wrote a set of articles between 1795 and 1798 in Latin under his Latin name Hechtius, i.e. two decades earlier than Jullien's. But as Lenhart posits, Hechtius's treatise is also characterised by a very different methodology:

> The two founding fathers led the ground for two different methodological approaches that can be pursued across the history of the discipline: an interpretive historical-philosophical-qualitative (Hecht) and a data-generating empirical-positivist-quantitative one (Jullien).

If the *four steps of comparison* model of Bereday and Hilker is placed into this broader debate, it can be characterised as an elaborated version of the 'interpretive historical-philosophical-qualitative' type, even though it might encompass quantitative data such as enrolment ratios or other factual data. This categorisation is in line with Manzon's view (2007, 86); she distinguishes between 'interpretive' and 'causal-analytic' purposes of comparison.

As an alternative to the interpretive model, the use of deductive reasoning and quantitative analyses and testing, such as PISA, has become more frequent in recent decades. This may lead to naive empiricism and result in normative and natural fallacies, for which

Jullien's vision may be criticised (Adick 2008, 24). However, these dangers are there in 'causal-analytic' as well as in 'interpretive' approaches.

The limitations of the *four steps* model, with respect to the number of cases or countries that can be treated, has led to new and different methodologies. In the meantime, even global comparisons have become 'normal'. They are widely practised and manageable not least owing to new information technologies and the rising impact of data collection in international organisations. Examples include the acquisition, processing, reporting and interpretation of enrolment statistics on a worldwide scale by the Education for All initiative under UNESCO. This resulted in a set of extensive *Global Monitoring Reports* (2000–2015), continued from 2016 as *Global Education Monitoring Reports*. Also, from an academic point of view, today, macro-level theories in respect of education worldwide may not only be formulated but can also be effectively and empirically tested as is demonstrated in the numerous research papers of the *world-polity approach* following John W. Meyer and others (Boli, Ramirez, and Meyer 1985; Meyer and Ramirez 2000). Their approach has been evaluated as predominantly quantitative not least through their preference for using existing data sets (e.g. from UN sources) in order to test hypotheses stemming from various macro-perspective theories on the relation between education and political, economic, cultural and other variables in the world (Adick 2009).

Research realities also often display a mix of approaches. For instance, findings from inductive studies are considered as pre-tests that lead to the heuristic formulation of theoretical assumptions then tested in a deductive research design. Secondary analysis is used in which results are arranged in a quasi-experimental way according to pre-defined variables and tested for significant effects. In his treatise on comparison, Hilker (1962, 106f) references the German philosopher Wilhelm Windelband. Known for his classification of science(s), Windelband suggests a distinction between *idiographic* sciences (culture research) which aim to *understand* the world and *nomothetic* sciences (nature research) which aim to *explain* the world. In Windelband's views, both are *empirical* sciences as opposed to *rational* sciences (mathematics and logic). He stressed that any research object in the empirical sciences is *not* taken from reality, but is always a scientific construction, and that research in empirical sciences will always use both idiographic and nomothetic ways of reasoning (Windelband 1914, §12, 229ff.).

Historically, comparative education – such as educational science in general and other social sciences – has adopted both these views. Hechtius aimed to understand the historical and societal context and ways in which education in England and Germany made sense in his times. Jullien was interested to discover and explain variables which guaranteed the functioning of nascent national education systems in Europe by means of questionnaires which he intended to circulate in various countries. Even today, the dichotomy 'idiographic vs. nomothetic' is seen as basic to the discipline and is canonised in introductory texts on comparative education (e.g. Parreira do Amaral 2015, 109–111). Seen from this perspective, the *four steps of comparison* model may be characterised as an idiographic approach which, however, and following Windelband, logically leads also to imply nomothetic reasoning. This is firmly established in Hilker's concept (1962, 126) which ends by referring to Bereday's (1961b) diagnosis of school reforms in France and Turkey – that both systems would be a copy of another model depending on a centralised education ministry; this could then be tested in further research under different circumstances. In his final discussion of 'total analysis', Bereday (1964, 25) also appeals to nomothetic reasoning in ascertaining that the final stage of comparative education as an academic discipline such as other social sciences 'is concerned with the formulation of "laws" or "typologies"'.

Overall, then, the *four steps of comparison* model *was* a valuable inductive methodology of its time, and *may still* guide scholars in constructing the basic steps of comparison of particular countries, in cases typical for academic examinations, acting in international collaboration, and in comparing a limited number of countries.

Notes

1. For an international readership, it should be added that in the history of comparative education in Germany, two terms were used for what is internationally known as 'comparative education'. Hilker deliberately used *Vergleichende Pädagogik* (*Comparative Pedagogy*) instead of *Vergleichende Erziehungswissenschaft*, as Friedrich Schneider (1961) chose to call this academic discipline, whereby *Educational Science* would be the adequate translation of the German *Erziehungswissenschaft* instead of just calling it 'education'. For details of his choice, cf. Hilker (1962, 142–143).
2. The *Arbeitsgruppe Internationale Vergleichsstudie* was coordinated by Eckhard Klieme (DIPF) and consisted of researchers from various universities and research institutions, among them Hans Döbert, Isabell van Ackeren, Wilfried Bos, Klaus Klemm, Rainer H. Lehmann, Botho von Kopp, Knut Schwippert, Wendelin Sroka and Manfred Weiß. The book has been in print and open access online for the public and has been reprinted several times.
3. The challenge came about when reading Manzon (2007), which overlapped with writing my *Introduction to Comparative Education* which was published in 2008.
4. The author thanks Oskar Anweiler for his communication on what he recalled about the relationship of Hilker and Bereday and in which languages Hilker was proficient. Anweiler supported the view that both of them got along well and respected each other's academic work, despite the generational gap and the historical challenges of the post-war situation. Anweiler also confirmed that, according to his recollection, Hilker was proficient in English and French but not in Russian or other (modern) languages (telephone interview, 2 November 2016).
5. Quotation from the German original:

   > Zuerst die Geographie der Erziehung, die systematische Sammlung pädagogischer Informationen in einem einzigen Land, dann ihre Analyse mit Hilfe der Begriffe der Sozialwissenschaften, danach der gleichzeitige Vergleich ausgewählter Probleme in verschiedenen Ländern und letztlich die totale vergleichende Analyse: diese vier Schritte der Verfahrensweise zeigen der Vergleichenden Pädagogik den Weg in die Zukunft.

6. For a short biography of Bereday, see the entry in the online *CIEclopedia*: http://www.nie.edu.sg/research/publication/cieclopedia-org/ [accessed 14 Oct.2016], in this source there is, however, no entry on Hilker. For a short biography of Hilker, see Steier (2012) in the *Klinkhardt Lexikon Erziehungswissenschaft*, in which, however, there is no entry on Bereday.
7. *George Z.F. Bereday Dead; Education, Author and Editor*. In the 'Obituaries' Section of the *New York Times* 26 October 1983.
8. For an overview of the history of these organisations, cf. Adick (2008, 24–29). Articles especially devoted to the CIES (Swing 2007), the CESE (Mitter 2007) and the German SIIVE (Waterkamp 2007) are also part of a collective work on the World Council of Comparative Education Societies edited by Vandra Masemann, Mark Bray and Maria Manzon (2007).
9. This obituary (one page and no author) was obviously written at short notice before the first number of 1969 of the journal went to the printer. It begins by stressing that Hilker, who died

on 4 January 1969, had still actively participated some weeks earlier in the meeting of the editorial group of 'his' journal.

10. Addressing the inductive nature of the *four steps of comparison* model is in line with the self-evaluation of Hilker who himself deliberately categorises and defends his methodological procedure as an 'inductive way of reasoning' in earlier articles (cf. Hilker 1957, 618).

11. While teaching comparative education, I often employed some simple but eye-opening examples to sensitise students to the traps of this basic fallacy: If we research some 10 or so countries and find that all or the great majority of them practise single-sex schooling (or other features like having compulsory education laws), it cannot be concluded that all education systems function like this. Also, it cannot be concluded that education systems *should* practise these things (the also very frequently occurring normative fallacy).

Disclosure statement

No potential conflict of interest was reported by the author.

References

Adick, Christel. 2008. *Vergleichende Erziehungswissenschaft. Eine Einführung*. Stuttgart: Kohlhammer.

Adick, Christel. 2009. "World Polity – ein Forschungsprogramm und Theorierahmen zur Erklärung weltweiter Bildungsentwicklungen." In *Neo-Institutionalismus in der Erziehungswissenschaft. Grundlegende Texte und empirische Studien*, edited by S. Koch and M. Schemmann, 258–291. Wiesbaden: VS. Verlag für Sozialwissenschaften.

Adick, Christel. 2014a. "Vergleichen – aber wie? Methodik und Methodologie in der Vergleichenden Erziehungswissenschaft." In *Methoden des Vergleichs – Komparatistische Methodologie und Forschungsmethodik in interdisziplinärer Perspektive*, edited by Christine Freitag, 15–38. Opladen: Budrich UniPress.

Adick, Christel. 2014b. "Der methodologische Nationalismus und Kulturalismus in der Vergleichenden Erziehungswissenschaft." In *Mehrsprachigkeit – Diversität – Internationalität. Erziehungswissenschaft im transnationalen Bildungsraum*, edited by S. Rühle, A. Müller, and P. D. T. Knobloch, 225–241. Münster: Waxmann.

Anweiler, Oskar. 1969. "Franz Hilker: In Memoriam." *Comparative Education* 5 (2): 121–123.

Anweiler, Oskar. 2013. "Franz Hilker – ein unverstellter Blick nach Osten. Eine Skizze." *Bildung und Erziehung* 66 (3): 321–330.

Arbeitsgruppe Internationale Vergleichsstudie. 2003. *Vertiefender Vergleich der Schulsysteme ausgewählter PISA-Teilnehmerstaaten*. Bonn: Bundesministerium für Bildung und Forschung.

Bereday, George Z. F. 1961a. "Theorie und Methoden der Vergleichenden Erziehungswissenschaft." In *Weltweite Erziehung. Als Festgabe für Friedrich Schneider zum 80. Geburtstag*, edited by W. Brezinka, 139–162. Freiburg: Herder.

Bereday, George Z. F. 1961b. "Schulreformen in Frankreich und der Türkei – Versuch einer systematischen Vergleichung." *Bildung und Erziehung* 14: 226–243.

Bereday, George Z. F. 1964. *Comparative Method in Education*. New York: Holt, Rinehart and Winston.

Bereday, George Z. F., William W. Brickman, and Gerald H. Read. 1960. *The Changing Soviet School*. Boston: Houghton Mifflin.

Boli, John, Francisco Ramirez, and John W. Meyer. 1985. "Explaining the Origins and Expansion of Mass Education." *Comparative Education Review* 29 (2): 145–170.

Bray, Mark. 2004. "Methodology and Focus in Comparative Education." In *Education and Society in Hong Kong and Macao: Comparative Perspectives on Continuity and Change*, edited by M. Bray and R. Koo, 237–350, 2nd ed., CERC Studies in Comparative Education 7. Hong Kong: Comparative Education Research Centre, The University of Hong Kong.

Brickman, William W. 1969. "Franz Hilker (1881-1969)." *Comparative Education Review* 13 (2): 149.

Garrido, García, and Jose Luis. 1996. *Fundamentos de Educación Comparada*. Madrid: Editorial Dykinson S.L.

Hilker, Franz. 1922. "Der Bildungsgedanke im neuen Rußland." *Die Neue Erziehung* 4: 186–191.

Hilker, Franz. 1928. "Pädagogische Amerikafahrt." *Pädagogisches Zentralblatt* 8: 528–533.

Hilker, Franz. 1957. "Zur theoretischen Grundlegung einer vergleichenden Pädagogik." *Bildung und Erziehung* 10: 482–491, 614–620.

Hilker, Franz. 1962. *Vergleichende Pädagogik*. München: Max Hueber.

Lenhart, Volker. Forthcoming. "Hechtius (1795–1798) - The Beginning of Historical-philosophical-idiographic Research in Comparative Education." *Comparative Education*.

Manzon, Maria. 2007. "Comparing Places." In *Comparative Education Research. Approaches and Methods*, edited by Mark Bray, Bob Adamson, and Mark Mason, 85–121. Hong Kong and Dordrecht: Comparative Education Research Centre, The University of Hong Kong and Springer.

Masemann, Vandra, Mark Bray, and Maria Manzon, eds. 2007. "Common Interests, Uncommon Goals." In *Histories of the World Council of Comparative Education Societies and Its Members*. Hong Kong and Dordrecht: Comparative Education Research Centre, The University of Hong Kong and Springer.

Meyer, John W., and Francisco O. Ramirez. 2000. "The World Institutionalization of Education." In *Discourse Formation in Comparative Education*, edited by Jürgen Schriewer, 111–132. Frankfurt: Lang.

Mitter, Wolfgang. 2007. "The Comparative Education Society in Europe (CESE)." In *Common Interests, Uncommon Goals. Histories of the World Council of Comparative Education Societies and Its Members*, edited by Vandra Masemann, Mark Bray, and Maria Manzon, 116–127. Hong Kong and Dordrecht: Comparative Education Research Centre, The University of Hong Kong and Springer.

Parreira do Amaral, Marcelo. 2015. "Methodologie und Methode in der International Vergleichenden Erziehungswissenschaft." In *Internationale und Vergleichende Erziehungswissenschaft. Geschichte, Theorie, Methode und Forschungsfelder*, edited by Marcelo Parreira do Amaral, and S. Karin Amos, 107–130. Münster: Waxmann.

Phillips, David, and Michele Schweisfurth. 2014. *Comparative and International Education: An Introduction to Theory, Method and Practice*. 2nd ed. London: Continuum.

Rothe, Georg. 2001. *Die Systeme beruflicher Qualifizierung Deutschlands, Österreichs und der Schweiz im Vergleich*. Villingen-Schwenningen: Neckar.

Schneider, Friedrich. 1961. *Vergleichende Erziehungswissenschaft. Geschichte. Forschung. Lehre*. Heidelberg: Quelle & Meyer.

Steier, Sonja. 2012. "Franz Hilker (1881–1969)." In *Klinkhardt Lexikon Erziehungswissenschaft*. 2 (44). Bad Heilbrunn: UTB Klinkhardt.

Stübig, Heinz. 1997. "Die Wiederbegründung der Vergleichenden Erziehungswissenschaft in Westdeutschland nach dem Zweiten Weltkrieg – Friedrich Schneider und Franz Hilker." *Bildung und Erziehung* 50: 467–480.

Swing, Elizabeth Sherman. 2007. "The Comparative and International Education Society (CIES)." In *Common Interests, Uncommon Goals. Histories of the World Council of Comparative Education Societies and Its Members*, edited by Vandra Masemann, Mark Bray, and Maria Manzon, 94–115. Hong Kong and Dordrecht: Comparative Education Research Centre, The University of Hong Kong and Springer.

Waterkamp, Dietmar. 2006. *Vergleichende Erziehungswissenschaft. Ein Lehrbuch*. Münster: Waxmann.

Waterkamp, Dietmar. 2007. "The Section for International and Intercultural Comparative Education in the German Society for Education." In *Common Interests, Uncommon Goals. Histories of the World Council of Comparative Education Societies and Its Members*, edited by Vandra Masemann, Mark Bray, and Maria Manzon, 139–154. Hong Kong and Dordrecht: Comparative Education Research Centre, The University of Hong Kong and Springer.

Windelband, Wilhelm. 1914. *Einleitung in die Philosophie*. Tübingen: J.C.B. Mohr.

The Nazi seizure of the *International Education Review*: a dark episode in the early professional development of comparative education

Erwin H. Epstein

ABSTRACT

It was not until the 1930s that comparative education, with the initiation of dedicated courses and programmes at universities in various countries, that the field became internationally recognised in its own right. And, it was not until the 1930s that the first internationally recognised journal in the field, the *International Education Review*, was founded by Friedrich Schneider of Germany. The journal's launch happened to be concurrent with the rise of Hitler. Once Hitler was appointed Chancellor of Germany in 1933, he initiated his purge of Jews and liberal democratic elements in the universities, and this action was felt soon afterwards by the *IER*. After overcoming early financial difficulties, the *IER* developed promisingly until 1934, when the Nazi ideologue, Alfred Bäumler, replaced Schneider shortly before Schneider was dismissed from his positions at the Academy of Pedagogics in Bonn and the University of Cologne. Bäumler's philosophy was one of virulent anti-Semitism and focused on the critical role to be played by the Aryan race in the Nazi master plan. This article is an account of how, in the mid-1930s, this same Nazi racist took charge of the *International Education Review*, which at that time was the most important international forum in comparative education.

We comparativists take well-deserved pride in the service we perform in behalf of world education. We are valued for the work we do by international organisations such as UNESCO, by ministries of education, and by the larger educational community. Most of us subscribe to the highest ideals of scholarship and social justice. Because of this, the intrusion of injustice surely disturbs those who view comparative education as a field with an academically impeccable and unassailable past.

Nevertheless, comparative education has on occasion been a fierce battlefield of rival ideologies regarding right and wrong. Consider, for example, the blanket demonisation of Western comparative education by Soviet comparativists during the Cold War. In their textbook on comparative education for use in the Soviet Union and Cuba, M.A. Soko-lova, E.H. Kuzmina, and M.L. Radionov (1978; in Spanish, 1982) claimed that 'bourgeois comparative education [has] the objective of falsifying [the Soviet Union's] fundamental principles, of weakening the resonance that the socialist countries have achieved the world over in the area of cultural and instructional development' (my translation from pp. 31–32 of the Spanish edition). However uncommon such vitriol may be, it is important to be aware of how those at the periphery of our field view the mainstream.

A sign of a field's maturity is its willingness to reflect on all aspects of its own past, viewing moments both of the sublime and of the depraved. There have been histories of comparative education, of course, but until recently these have been mainly on devel-opments within particular countries or regions (good examples are Brickman 1966 and 1977 in regard to the U.S., and Velloso 1989, with respect to Spain). *Common Interests, Uncommon Goals: Histories of the World Council of Comparative Education Societies and Its Members* (Masemann, Bray, and Manzon 2007) is one that comprehensively looks at the structure of comparative education as a field and analyzes how that structure evolved. Other comparable histories include *Comparative Education at Universities World Wide* (Wolhuter et al. 2013) and *Crafting a Global Field: Six Decades of the Comparative and International Education Society* (Epstein 2016b). These comprehensive volumes contain occasional descriptions of suppression. For example, Crain Soudien (2007) writes about the distrust of comparativists of education under the apartheid state of South Africa, Nikolay Popov (2013) refers to 'ideological monism' under communism in Bulgaria, and Erwin H. Epstein (2016a) shows how early leaders of the Comparative and International Education Society attempted to enlighten others about the consequences to education under Nazi and Soviet domination. Nevertheless, these histories are mostly celebratory; accounts of the darker side of comparative education are relatively rare. This article probes undoubtedly the darkest period of the field's past, when comparative education faced the threat of Nazi depredation and dominance.

The context

One of the most deeply troubling conclusions about the greatest crime of the twentieth century – I refer, of course, to the mass murder of millions of innocent people by the Nazis in the 1930s and 1940s – is that it was abetted by many intellectuals in a variety of academic fields. This was not a crime largely of the poor and desperate, but one that drew from the ranks of all social classes and was driven by an ideological engine forged with the aid of scholars.

In the universal struggle between good and evil, perhaps no two traits stand out on the side of the good as much as democracy and education. Yet democracy has occasionally given rise to terrorists and despots. Witness, for example, the democratic election of the Hamas government in Gaza and that of Robert Mugabe in Zimbabwe. Similarly, with regard to education, demonic extremist teaching in some Wahabbi madrasas has bred vicious fanatics. The faith we have in education and democracy, as symbolised by the slogan 'Education for All', is sorely tested by school-taught extremism and fanaticism. Indeed, the fear of extremism in education has become so strong in the Western democ-racies that it is being pitted against the cherished principles of academic freedom and the free expression of self and ideas. Consider, for example, the banning of religious articles of clothing in French schools stemming from the militant separation of church and state in that country (Kilinç 2014) and the argument by the U.K.'s Joint Committee on Human Rights that to require universities to prevent people from being drawn to terrorism would stifle academic freedom (Human Rights Joint Report 2015).

Neither democracy nor education is an unalloyed good, having produced on occasion both anti-democratic consequences and individuals whose minds are closed to all but a narrow ideology. Unfortunate outcomes of democracy and education, however sporadic they may be, have persisted especially since the rise of Nazism – surely the greatest tyranny of the twentieth century. The appointment of Adolf Hitler in 1933 as a Chancellor of Germany under a democratically elected government and the Nazi use of education as an instrument of cruelty and injustice are enduring reminders of how the outcomes of democracy and of education are not always favourable.

In a country that produced some of the greatest minds in history, Germany was a per-plexing host of Nazi despotism. It is especially strange that under that despotic rule, it was not only undereducated thugs who engaged in wanton acts of evil but the intellectual elite as well. To be sure, the Nazis, through a system of public works projects and pump priming brought economic relief during a severe depression, and in this way won over the allegiance of many (Allen 1973). And, complicity in Nazi depredation came from various sectors, including elements of the Catholic Church (Brown-Fleming 2005) and Pro-testant denominations (Trachtenberg 1986; Goldhagen 1996). Yet without the intellectual foundation of Nazi thought advanced by university professors in a wide range of fields, the ideology of racial and political hatred could not have taken hold. The blessings bestowed on Nazism by many academics gave fascists much of the justification they needed to con-vince the masses that exercising a sense of Nazi superiority was morally correct. The mandate given to the Nazis by intellectuals expedited political allegiance to the Nazi regime and allowed extreme racism to penetrate mass consciousness. If our finest thinkers believe that racial savagery is proper and moral, so many less educated mortals reasoned, such behaviour must be not merely permissible but obligatory (Goldhagen 1996; Overy 2005). Practitioners in many scholarly fields gave sanction to Nazi brutality, either by indif-ference or through active discourse. This is equally true of comparative education. Can we thus exonerate our own field? This question underlies the focus of this article.

Scholarship in the service of Nazi ideology

A proper view of the role of comparative education in the Nazi quest for domination must take into account the overall state of scholarship under Nazi rule. Indeed, intellectual support for Nazi ideology came from virtually all academic disciplines – from philosophy to physics, from biology to art and music, and from anthropology to history. Scientists in the 1930s denounced the 'theoretical formalism' of anti-*Volk* Jewish science. The very pol-itical process of creating a unified Germany was based on the exclusionary racial purity concept of the *Volk*. This racist notion of a pure Germanic people, rooted in nineteenth-century anti-Semitic writings, was abetted by many intellectuals and became widespread. Nobel Prize winner physicist Johannes Stark insistently opposed Albert Einstein's postu-late, central to his theory of relativity, that 'all observers in the universe were equivalent and symmetrical'. Rather, Stark claimed that 'privileged intuition' was the only legitimate source of knowledge, with 'privilege' being an exclusively *völkisch* property. Another physicist and Nobel laureate, Philipp Lenard, was given an award by the notorious Nazi propagandist, Alfred Rosenberg, for teaching a 'German Physics (Deutsche Physik)' as opposed to Einstein's 'Jewish physics' (Mason 1975; Beyerchen 1977; Weinrich 1999).

The most notorious examples of professorial complicity are to be found in medicine and the physical sciences. Besides the involvement of physicists and engineers in the development of advanced armaments, professors of psychiatry like Carl Schneider at the University of Heidelberg and Max de Crinis at the University of Berlin helped to shape the Nazi euthanasia policy and, in fact, chose death for many psychiatric patients. Physical anthropologists collaborated by categorising the worthiness of humans, so that Polish children with blond hair and 'Aryan' heads were forcibly sent west for 'Germanisation'. Those deemed purely Polish were shipped to work camps, and Jews and Roma were sent to death camps (Schafft 2005). More pertinent to the pervasive spread of Nazi consciousness, however, were the disciplines of history, philosophy, and the social sciences. Hans Sluga (1993, 8) reports that about half of all of Germany's philosophers, including the illustrious Martin Heidegger, became members of the Nazi Party. Indeed, eight of the 14 men who, at the Wannsee Conference in 1942, advanced the mass murder of Jews held doctorate degrees from the finest universities of Central Europe (Patterson 1996).

Altogether, the university professoriate in Germany in 1933, the year Hitler rose to power, were a relatively small group, numbering about 5000 individuals. Yet their influence in advancing anti-democratic sentiments went well beyond their small number. In a careful study of German universities during the Nazi period, Michael Grüttner (2005) concludes that the position of the majority of university professors towards having a democratic republic was 'from the outset one of rejection or at least pronounced distance' (p. 78). This rejectionist attitude was interlaced with *völkisch* anti-Semitism, displayed more by open discrimination against Jewish candidates for professorial chairs than by rampant verbal aggression. Indeed, prior to the rise of Nazism, almost 10 per cent of Prussian university instructors were Jews, about 10 times their percentage in the overall population. Yet, within only a few months after Hitler was appointed Chancellor of Germany, mass dismissals of Jews and others who refused to welcome the new regime were accepted with virtually no protest from their colleagues (Remy 2000).

With a complicit professoriate, *völkisch* ideology became institutionalised with the introduction of such new fields as racial science (*Rassenkunde*), racial hygiene (*Rassenhygiene*), and Nazi interpretations of folklore (*Volkskunde*). Among the most influential academic movements during this period was the *Ostforschung*, research on the East, initially advanced mainly by a small group of young historians, sociologists, and demographers who viewed the *Volk* community of blood rather than the German national state as the centre of history (Burleigh 1988). Aly and Heim (2002) show how academic followers of *Ostforschung*, intimately infused with the idea of *völkisch* superiority, gave intellectual sanction to the Holocaust. Ingo Haar and Michael Fahlbusch reveal how the racial ethnic 'scholarship' of historians, such as Hans Rothfels, Theodor Scheider, Werner Conze, and Hermann Aubin, found direct application in the Nazi deportation and extermination of hundreds of thousands of Poles and Jews (Fahlbusch 2005; Haar 2005).

Indeed, the very platform of Nazi ideology was tied to the concept of the *Volk*. Although Nazi ideologues were united in viewing the *Volk* as a community bound together by blood, there was some disagreement about the extent to which that community should be defined primarily in racial terms. Some, like Heidegger, believed in the primacy of the

Volk's spirituality, although he certainly did not exclude its racial character (Bernasconi 2000). Yet others, in particular Alfred Bäumler, elevated the importance of race above all else. Bäumler's philosophy was indeed one of virulent anti-Semitism and focused on the critical role to be played by the Aryan race in the Nazi master plan. In the mid-1930s, this same Nazi racist took charge of the *International Education Review*, which at that time was the most important international forum in comparative education.

The rise and fall of the *International Education Review*

The roots of comparative education can be found deep in the nineteenth century with the appearance of works of such precursors as Marc-Antoine Jullien de Paris, Victor Cousin, Horace Mann, and Matthew Arnold. Yet, a professional academic field cannot arise until a group of adherents view themselves as having a common ground of knowledge through formal association and a shared sense of responsibility to convey that knowledge to others.

It was not until the turn of the twentieth century and afterwards that such formal association was displayed by the emergence of courses, intellectual centres, and publications dedicated to the field. The first comparative education course ever taught in higher education was probably given in the U.S. at Teachers College, Columbia University by James Russell in 1898–1899 (Bereday 1964), and the first centre for comparative education, also at Teachers College, called the International Institute, was formed in 1923, with Paul Monroe as Director and four other faculty members, among whom was Isaac Kandel (Bu 1997). Publication forums for general consumption began in the post-World War I period with the appearance of Peter Sandiford's edited volume entitled *Comparative Education* (1918) and *The Educational Yearbook*, which was initiated in 1924 under Kandel's editorship. However, it was not until the 1930s that comparative education, with the initiation of dedicated courses and programmes at universities in various countries, that the field became internationally recognised in its own right. And, it was not until the 1930s that the first internationally recognised journal in the field, the *International Education Review*, was established.

Launching the *International Education Review*

An academic journal serves several purposes that are critical to the wellbeing and stability of a professional field. Normally issued several times during the year, it keeps practitioners informed of important research. It sets scholarly norms and boundaries as well as standards of quality. And, it gives those with common interests a sense of identity about their field. In 1930, Friedrich Schneider of Germany founded the first scholarly journal in comparative education, the *International Education Review* (*IER*). He was joined soon afterwards by Paul Monroe as co-editor when the journal's first issue was published in 1931 in Cologne. Thus, the *IER* was produced collaboratively by Germany's leading comparativist of the time together with, in the U.S., the founder of the world's first comparative education centre. Indeed, given that the *IER* represented the first formal collaboration of leading comparativists across continents, its editorship marked the launching of comparative education as an international field. As such, it was hailed as 'this new enterprise in international understanding' by such luminaries as George Counts, the radical progressive whose provocative speeches were about to be published as a widely debated book, *Dare the School Build a New Social Order* (1932); Stephen Duggan, Director of the Institute of International Education; and Franz Hilker, who, next to Schneider, was the most prominent German comparativist of the time (*International Education Review* 1931/2, 11–12).

In view of the editors' standing as among the world's most eminent comparativists, and the acclaim the journal received upon its launch, there was ample reason for optimism. Schneider more than any other scholar was responsible for bringing forward Wilhelm Dilthey's concept of *Triebkräfte*, or forces affecting education, into comparative education epistemology (see Epstein and Carroll 2005). Monroe had abundant editorial experience, having been editor-in-chief of the five-volume *Cyclopedia of Education* (1910–1913), and, as mentioned earlier, was the founding director of the first centre for comparative education, the International Institute at Teachers College, Columbia University in New York City.

Unfortunately, Germany proved to be an uncongenial venue for starting the new enterprise. Both Schneider and Monroe were ardent activists in promoting democracy through education and believed that educational contact was, in Monroe's words, '[of] the greatest advantage … in cultivating international understanding and good will' ('Speech of 1924'; quoted in Bu 1997, 415). However, the journal's launch happened to be concurrent with the rise of Hitler. Once Hitler was appointed Chancellor of Germany in 1933, he initiated his purge of Jews and liberal democratic elements in the universities, and this action was felt soon afterwards by the *IER*. After overcoming early financial difficulties, the *IER* developed promisingly until 1934, when the Nazi ideologue, Alfred Bäumler, replaced Schneider shortly before Schneider was dismissed from his positions at the Pedagogical Academy in Bonn and the University of Cologne.

Bäumler was appointed not by an editorial or governing board associated with the journal itself, nor was the appointment made by virtue of his university affiliation. Rather, he was made co-editor by the Nazi authorities, in particular by the notorious Alfred Rosenberg, who was hanged as a war criminal at Nuremburg by the Allies after World War II. Rosenberg's most famous work was *The Myth of the Twentieth Century* (*Der Mythus des 20 Jahrhunderts*), which sold over a million copies and had an influence in Germany comparable to that of Hitler's *Mein Kampf*. Rosenberg incorporated the racial theories of Joseph-Arthur de Gobineau and Houston Stewart Chamberlain to contend that race was the decisive factor in the course of world history. In regard especially to education, he worked closely with and drew ideas from Bäumler.

Soon after Hitler rose to power in 1933, Bäumler became Chair of Political Education at Berlin University as well as Head of the academic division of Rosenberg's Office for the Surveillance of the Whole Intellectual and Ideological Education and Training of the National Socialist Party. In these capacities, Bäumler played a key role in developing and conveying Nazi philosophy. Hans Sluga (1993, 127) characterises Bäumler as 'more than any other German philosopher, the typical fascist intellectual'. Lisa Harries calls Bäumler 'perhaps the most prominent philosopher to identify with National Socialism' (Harries 1990, 268). David Pan shows that Bäumler developed his ideas into 'a theoretical justification for racism and a practical program for Nazi pedagogy' (Pan 2001, 42). Moreover, Frank H.W. Edler claims that Bäumler introduced 'the grammar of war into every aspect of the educational system' (Edler 1999: Part I, p. 11). Within weeks after Hitler came to power, libraries were 'cleansed' of works by Jewish authors, and, in an act he viewed as moral purification,

Bäumler, immediately after giving his inaugural address as Chair of Political Education at the University of Berlin, led his Nazi students to a site where they engaged in the infamous burning of banned books. Clearly, Bäumler was no ordinary scholar: he, Rosenberg, and Ernst Krieck were the individuals most responsible for crafting and intellectually legitimising Nazi racist ideology.

The infusion of Nazi ideology

Once Bäumler became co-editor, the tenor of the *IER* changed gradually but perceptibly. Unsurprisingly, Bäumler early on injected racist content into the journal, bringing on as authors some of the most virulent anti-Semites, such as Ernst Krieck (1933-4, 309–313). A professor at Frankfurt-am-Main who later rose to be rector of the University of Heidelberg, Krieck became a member of the SS, the elite unit of the Nazi Party that murdered millions of Jews, Poles, Roma, and Russians. He envisioned a unified *völkisch*-political worldview in which all personal aspirations, class prejudices, and religious differences would be submerged into a National Socialist *Volk* communal form of life (Bambach 2003, 95, 128).

With the 1935 edition, publication of the *IER* moved from Cologne to Berlin, the city in which Bäumler worked and where he could maintain tighter control of the journal. In the first issue published from Berlin, German Reichsminister of Education Bernhard Rust gave introductory remarks expressing his best wishes for the journal's success. That issue included an article by the young Nazi scholar Bernhard Holfelder who wrote that

> it would be a grateful task to develop the system of National Socialist pedagogy out of the manifold forms of National Socialist educational reality. Such a pedagogy can indeed become an object of science like the whole phenomenon of education … (Holfelder 1935, 12)

Holfelder would later become Head of the Office of Education under Reichminister Rust.

Of course, the Nazi thrust into comparative education with the *IER* as its instrument caused dismay in the rest of the comparative education world, especially in the U.S., where Paul Monroe served as the journal's co-editor. This raises the question of why Monroe stayed on despite Schneider's dismissal and the atrocities and threats to academic freedom that were being reported out of Germany. Why indeed, did he not try to move the journal to the U.S.? Further research needs to be done to answer these questions, but we can speculate about his reasons.

For one thing, it is important to understand that the disturbing events in Germany were couched in terms unfamiliar to the Americans. Despite the outrages committed by the Nazis from the moment Hitler was appointed to office, it was not intellectually easy for outsiders to make sense of what the Nazis were up to, with their use of highly obscure language and concepts that appeared even more muddled when translated into English. This difficulty of comprehension was certainly not limited to the American readers of the *IER*, but applied to the American academy generally.

For another thing, institutional anti-Semitism, common in many American universities at the time, might have lessened the impact of Nazi depravity on the consciousness of American academics. Ido Oren (2002) reports that prominent American political scientists during the 1930s maintained that the Nazi regime was not without positive achievements, especially in the area of public administration, and that Americans could learn from those achievements. Stephen H. Norwood, in an exhaustive analysis of Harvard University's reaction to Hitler's rise, contends:

> In warmly welcoming Nazi leaders to the Harvard campus, inviting them to prestigious, high-profile social events, and striving to build friendly relations with thoroughly Nazified universities in Germany, while denouncing those who protested against these actions, Harvard's administration and many of its student leaders offered important encouragement to the Hitler regime as it intensified its persecution of Jews and expanded its military strength. (Norwood 2004, 189)

For example, in 1936 Harvard President James Bryant Conant sent a delegate to the 550th anniversary celebration of Heidelberg University, an institution thoroughly under Nazi control. By the time of the celebration, Heidelberg had dismissed dozens of faculty members for 'racial, religious, or political reasons', and had become one of the two principal centres for the propagation of 'Aryan Physics' and the removal of 'Jewish science'. Heidelberg's medical faculty promoted 'racial hygiene', sterilising people they considered 'defective', and were involved in the systematic slaughter of people they deemed mentally ill and handicapped.

Harvard was not alone in feting Nazi academics. Twenty American universities accepted invitations to send delegates to the Heidelberg celebration, among them Columbia University, where Paul Monroe had been director of the International Institute. Indeed, prior to the Heidelberg celebration, Columbia President Nicholas Murray Butler carried on an active correspondence with his counterparts at Harvard and Yale about how to deflect criticism of their decision to send delegates to the Nazi festival. In response to a student protest at his mansion demanding that he not send a delegate, President Butler expelled the leader of the students from the university (Norwood 2004, 215). It is plausible that Monroe interpreted Butler's actions as favouring cooperation with the Nazis, and that as a Columbia faculty member he felt obliged to follow along accordingly. By clear contrast, Britain's preeminent universities, Oxford and Cambridge, along with Manchester, Liverpool, Birmingham, London, Edinburgh and Dublin, refused invitations to send delegates to the Heidelberg celebration because of the outrages committed by that university.

It was important to Bäumler that the *IER* maintain its international currency, and he was clever enough to keep from flooding the journal with articles filled with Nazi ideology. He was also intent on keeping Monroe interested in staying on as co-editor for as long as possible. The Nazis, after all, had their own educational journals for internal consumption, such as Krieck's *Volk im Werden*, filled with their depraved racist ideology. The *IER*, with its international reputation and internationally shared editorship, represented for them a powerful vehicle to enlighten the world with their ideas while limiting suspicion of their malevolent intent. Bäumler's strategy here was a common one used by Nazi scholars concerned with maintaining an international stature. Holger Dainat (1994, 565ff; as cited by Grüttner 2005, 107) finds that 'especially those scholars who felt part of an international scientific community were generally at pains to avoid concessions to Nazi ideology in academic publications, since these would invariably diminish their reputations among foreign colleagues'. To maintain the *IER*'s international stature, Bäumler acted delicately, keeping to his racist principles but not excessively overstepping his boundaries with Monroe.

By the same token, Monroe was desperately trying to keep the journal alive and, at the same time, defend it from afar as best as he could against the Nazi incursion. He struggled, walking a tight line between accommodating to the perverse regime and sticking to the principle of academic freedom. In an editorial for the first issue of the *IER* after it had moved to Berlin, using words that reflected tortuous thinking, he wrote (Monroe 1935, 2):

> As in the field of politics sound internationalism can be based only on sound nationalism, so in the field of culture and in the teaching of culture, that is education, can worthwhile and significant international relations and contacts be built only upon fuller and more significant national education, activities and interests . . .

> As I understand the design of the 'International Education Review,' it is not concerned at all in decreasing the interest or enthusiasm which any national educators may have in their own education, nor is it interested in the promulgation of any set of ideas of any group of adherents, nor in any system or technique of education peculiar to any one country, or to any one large group of people.

Monroe's balancing act is clearly shown in the disparity of messages conveyed in these paragraphs. In the first paragraph, Monroe's words are those of appeasement, granting to the Nazis the importance of nationalism in education. By contrast, the second paragraph, while acknowledging the importance of educators having enthusiasm for their own national education, insists on a framework for the *IER* that opposes the advancement of ideas exclusive to any particular group or nation.

Unfortunately, Monroe was unable to sustain his balancing act for very long, and by 1938 he had had enough. He was replaced as co-editor by another American, the less distinguished Isaac Doughton, Dean of Instruction at State Teachers College in Mansfield, Pennsylvania. Two years later, with the 1940 edition, Bäumler became sole editor, and Nazi control became completely transparent. With the advent of war and the loss of a co-editor from abroad, the journal lost whatever little global credibility it had previously retained. In 1942, on the occasion of the 11th year of publication, Bäumler, with Theodor Wilhelm, wrote in an editorial,

> We could not find a better way to begin the new decennium [of publication] than with an article about the German Paul de Lagarde, to whom Europe is indebted for making clear the principle that the best and most enduring achievements are always those in which a nation has remained true to its original racial and historical forces, and that the character which arises from these forces is the only kind that is culturally productive. (Bäumler and Wilhelm 1942, 1, translated from German)

Lagarde, the individual whom Bäumler and Wilhelm were acclaiming, was a violent nineteenth-century anti-Semite whose writings were foundational to Alfred Rosenberg's Nazi ideology. Lagarde argued that Germany should create a 'national' form of Christianity, purged of Semitic elements, and insisted that Jews were 'pests and parasites' who should be destroyed 'as speedily and thoroughly as possible' (Snyder 1998, 203).

After the war, the *IER* sought to regain its intellectual footing. It was returned to Friedrich Schneider, was renumbered, and was moved from Berlin to Salzburg, Austria. A complete break with the past came in 1955, when the name of the journal was changed to the *International Review of Education* (*IRE*). It was again renumbered and returned to Germany, but with a difference. By this time, Schneider had moved back to Germany and shared a new international co-editorship with Karl W. Bigelow in New York, Roger Gal in Paris, M.J.

Langeveld in Utrecht, and Walther Merck in Hamburg. In addition, an international board of editorial consultants was appointed to guide the newly reconstituted journal. Most importantly, as noted in the first editorial of the refashioned journal, 'the fact that the Review is a foundation by the UNESCO Institute for Education in Hamburg guarantees its independence, worldwide character and freedom from nationalistic bias'.

The editors of the new *IRE*, however, displayed a convenient and extraordinary lapse of memory by also writing in that first editorial: 'Through Prof. Friedrich Schneider, who has shared in its establishment and serves as a member of its editorial board, [the *IRE*] may claim a connection with the pre-War *International Education Review* (1931–34)' (International Review of Education 1955, 1–2). For Schneider and the new editors, it was as if the *IER* expired at the end of 1934, with the subsequent years under the Nazis erased from all memory. That the *IER* was sustained for years after Schneider was removed as co-editor in 1934 is a real part of the history of comparative education, however unpalatable that chapter of history may be.

It took 2½ decades to launch the first truly international forum, as we know it today, in comparative education. It was a fitful and inauspicious start for such a worthy enterprise. However regrettable may be the episode described here, it should not be swept from historical memory. A strength of comparative education is its capacity to withstand the harsh light of intellectual scrutiny.

Conclusion

There is almost nothing in the comparative education literature about the episode described in this article. None of the histories of the field, at least in English, contain mention of it. It is not found in Brickman (1960); in Bereday (1964); in Noah and Eckstein (1969); in Wilson (1994); in Masemann, Bray, and Manzon (2007); or in any of the other comprehensive accounts of the field. In fact, these accounts generally ignore the very existence of the *International Education Review*, though it was the first internationally recognised journal in the field. It is as if we have had a collective case of memory loss.

Why is it important to remember such episodes? Let me advance three reasons. First, it is because memory forms identity. We are, after all, the sum total of our past memories and future aspirations. Just as a house cannot stand without a foundation, so an academic field cannot rightfully contemplate a meaningful future without grasping the fullness of its past. Any event that is not recorded and not remembered is as if it did not happen.

Second, revulsion towards the knowledge that our own field was complicit in the Nazi project is no reason to ignore the event. When viewed from the overall context of the time, in fact, we have much to be proud of. Complicity is only part of the picture – to be sure, the part that is mainly told in this article. However, it is important to look also at the other part, that is, the vigorous role that leading comparativists played early on to oppose Nazi depredation. I contend, indeed, that comparative education, as small a field as it was, did disproportionately more than other fields to resist the Nazis and awaken the world to the coming onslaught. Well before Hermann Rauschning (1939) issued his famous courageous warning to both his fellow Germans and to those outside Germany about the disastrous course the Nazi Party was taking, Friedrich Schneider had opposed the Nazis and tried to protect the *IER* at the cost of his own position. Isaac Kandel (1935), arguably the most important figure in twentieth-century comparative education (at least after his mentor, Michael Sadler), was astonishingly prescient in his early systematic assessment of German education as a tool to advance virulent Nazi totalitarianism. To forget the entire episode connecting comparative education to the Nazi project is to lose sight of the critical role that the field played in resisting Nazi perversion.

Finally, by ignoring the event we miss lessons to be learned. The most important lesson here is that we must not take for granted that our field is perforce free of doctrinaire intentions. Clearly, how we structure our activities affects how well we avoid ideological hegemony. The very existence of a multiplicity of journals and other forums in comparative education – so that no one publication can set a universal agenda for scholarship – serves that end. Being limited to only a few forums to function as scholarly outlets, as we were in the 1930s, creates a level of vulnerability that we should never again abide.

Disclosure statement

No potential conflict of interest was reported by the author.

References

Allen, William Sheridan. 1973. *The Nazi Seizure of Power: The Experience of a Single German Town, 1930–1935*. New York: New Viewpoints.

Aly, Götz, and Susanne Heim. 2002. *Architects of Annihilation: Auschwitz and the Logic of Destruction*. Princeton, NJ: Princeton University Press.

Bambach, Charles. 2003. *Heidegger's Roots: Nietzsche, National Socialism, and the Greeks*. Ithaca, NY: Cornell University Press.

Bäumler, Alfred, and Theodor Wilhelm. 1942. "Editorial." *International Education Review* 11: 1.

Bereday, George Z. F. 1964. *Comparative Method in Education*. New York: Rinehart & Winston.

Bernasconi, Robert. 2000. "Heidegger's Alleged Challenge to the Nazi Concept of Race." In *Appropriating Heidegger*, edited by James E. Faulconer and Mark A. Wrathall, 50–67. Cambridge: Cambridge University Press.

Beyerchen, Alan D. 1977. *Scientists under Hitler: Politics and the Physics Community in the Third Reich*. New Haven, CT: Yale University Press.

Brickman, William W. 1960. "A Historical Introduction to Comparative Education." *Comparative Education Review* 3 (February): 6–13.

Brickman, William W. 1966. "Ten Years of the Comparative Education Society." *Comparative Education Review* 10 (February): 4–15.

Brickman, William W. 1977. "Comparative and International Education Society: An Historical Analysis." *Comparative Education Review* 21 (June-October): 396–404.

Brown-Fleming, Suzanne. 2005. *The Holocaust and Catholic Conscience: Cardinal Aloisius Muench and the Guilt Question in Germany*. South Bend, IN: Notre Dame Press.

Bu, Liping. 1997. "International Activism and Comparative Education: Pioneering Efforts of the International Institute of Teachers College, Columbia University." *Comparative Education Review* 41 (November): 413–434.

Burleigh, Michael. 1988. *Germany Turns Eastward: A Study of Ostforschung in the Third Reich*. Cambridge: Cambridge University Press.

Counts, George S. 1932. *Dare the Schools Build a New Social Order*. New York: John Day.

Dainat, Holger. 1994. "'Wir müssen ja trotzdem weiter arbeiten' Die Deutsche Vierteljahrsschrift vor und nach 1945." *Deutsche Vierteljahrsschrift für Literaturwissenschaft und Geistesgeschichte* 68: 562–582.

Edler, Frank H. W. 1999. "Alfred Baeumler on Hölderlin and the Greeks: Reflections on the Heidegger-Baeumler Relationship." *Janus Head* (Online at http://www.janushead.org/JHspg99/edler.cfm)

Epstein, Erwin H. 2016a. "Early Leaders: Isaac Kandel, William W. Brickman, and C. Arnold Anderson." In *Crafting a Global Field: Six Decades of the Comparative and International Education Society*, edited by Erwin H. Epstein, 197–208. Hong Kong and Dordrecht: Comparative Education Research Centre, The University of Hong Kong and Springer.

Epstein, Erwin H., ed. 2016b. *Crafting a Global Field: Six Decades of the Comparative and International Education Society*. Hong Kong: Comparative Education Research Centre, The University of Hong Kong and Springer.

Epstein, Erwin H., and Katherine T. Carroll. 2005. "Abusing Ancestors: Historical Functionalism and the Postmodern Deviation in Comparative Education." *Comparative Education Review* 49 (February): 62–88.

Fahlbusch, Michael. 2005. "The Role and Impact of German Ethnopolitical Experts in the SS Reich Security Main Office." In *German Scholars and Ethnic Cleansing: 1919–1945*, edited by Ingo Haar and Michael Fahlbusch, 28–50. New York: Berghahn.

Faulkner, William. 1951. *Requiem for a Nun*. New York: Random House.

Goldhagen, Daniel J. 1996. *Hitler's Willing Executioners: Ordinary Germans and the Holocaust*. New York: Alfred A. Knopf.

Grüttner, Michael. 2005. "German Universities under the Swastika." In *Universities under Dictatorship*, edited by J. Connelly and M. Grüttner, 75–111. University Park, CA: Penn State Press.

Haar, Ingo. 2005. "German *Ostforschung* and Anti-Semitism." In *German Scholars and Ethnic Cleansing: 1919–1945*, edited by Ingo Haar and Michael Fahlbusch, 1–27. New York: Berghahn.

Harries, Lisa. 1990. Translator's Note 21 in Martin Heidegger, "The Rectorate 1933/34: Facts and Thoughts." In *Martin Heidegger and National Socialism: Questions and Answers*, edited by G. Neske and E. Kettering, 268. New York: Paragon House.

Holfelder, Bernhard. 1935. ""Das Ende der normativen Pädagogik." (The End of Normative Pedagogy). *International Education Review* 4: 5–12.

Human Rights Joint Committee - Fifth Report. 2015. *Legislative Scrutiny: Counter-Terrorism and Security Bill*. London: U.K. House of Lords and House of Commons, 7 January.

International Education Review. 1931/2. 1: 11–12.

International Review of Education. 1955. 1: 1–2.

Kandel, Isaac. 1935. *The Making of Nazis*. Westwood, CT: Greenwood.

Kilinç, Ramazan. 2014. "International Context and State-Religion Regimes in France and Turkey." In *Religion and Regimes: Support, Separation, and Opposition*, edited by Mehran Tamadonfar, and Ted G. Jelen, 97–120. Lexington Books: Plymouth.

Krieck, Ernst. 1933-4. "The Education of a Nation from Blood and Soil." *International Education Review* 3: 309–313.

Masemann, Vandra, Mark Bray, and Maria Manzon, eds. 2007. *Common Interests, Uncommon Goals: Histories of the World Council of Comparative Education Societies and Its Members*. Hong Kong: Springer and Comparative Education Research Centre, University of Hong Kong.

Mason, Stephen F. 1975. *A History of Science*. New York: Macmillan.

Monroe, Paul. 1935. "Editorial." *International Education Review* 4: 2.

Noah, Harold J., and Max A. Eckstein. 1969. *Toward a Science of Comparative Education*. London: Macmillan.

Norwood, Stephen H. 2004. "Legitimating Nazism: Harvard University and the Hitler Regime, 1933–1937." *American Jewish History* 92 (June): 189–223.

Oren, Ido. 2002. *Our Enemies and US: America's Rivalries and the Making of Political Science*. Ithaca, NY: Cornell University Press.

Overy, Richard. 2005. *The Dictators: Hitler's Germany, Stalin's Russia*. New York: W.W. Norton.

Pan, David. 2001. "Revising the Dialectic of Enlightenment: Alfred Baeumler and the Nazi Appropriation of Myth." *New German Critique* 84 (Fall): 37–50.

Patterson, David. 1996. *When Learned Men Murder*. Bloomington, IN: Phi Delta Kappa.

Popov, Nikolay. 2013. "Comparative Education in Bulgaria." In *Comparative Education at Universities Worldwide*, edited by Charl Wolhuter, N. Popov, B. Leutwyler, and K. S. Ermene, 29–36. Sofia: Bulgarian Comparative Education Society & University of Ljubljana Faculty of Arts.

Rauschning, Hermann. 1939. *The Revolution of Nihilism: Warning to the West*. New York: Alliance Book Corporation. Translated from the German by E. W. Dickes.

Remy, Steven P. 2000. *The Heidelberg Myth: The Nazification and Denazification of a German University*. Cambridge: Harvard University Press.

Sandiford, Peter, ed. 1918. *Comparative Education*. New York: Dutton.

Schafft, Gretchen E. 2005. *From Racism to Genocide: Anthropology in the Third Reich*. Champaign: University of Illinois Press.

Sluga, Hans. 1993. *Heidegger's Crisis: Philosophy and Politics in Nazi Germany*. Cambridge: Harvard University Press.

Snyder, Louis. 1998. "Paul de Lagarde." In *Encyclopedia of the Third Reich*, 203. Hertfordshire: Wordsworth.

Sokolova, M. A., E. H. Kuzima, and M. L. Radionaov. 1982. *Pedagogía Comparada*. Havana: Ministerio de Educación. Original version in Russian published in the U.S.S.R. (Editorial Prosvseshenie, 1978).

Soudien, Crain. 2007. "The Southern African Comparative and History of Education Society." In *Common Interests, Uncommon Goals: Histories of the World Council of Comparative Education Societies and Its Members*, edited by Vandra Masemann, Mark Bray, and María Manzon, 284–292. Hong Kong and Dordrecht: Comparative Education Research Centre, The University of Hong Kong and Springer.

Trachtenberg, Joshua. 1986. *The Devil and the Jews: The Medieval Conception of the Jew and Its Relation to Modern Anti-Semitism*. Philadelphia: Jewish Publication Society.

Velloso, Agustín de Santiesteban. 1989. *La Educación Comparada en España (1900–1936)*. Madrid: Universidad Nacional de Educación a Distancia.

Weinrich, Max. 1999. *Hitler's Professors*. New Haven: Yale University Press.

Wilson, David N. 1994. "Comparative and International Education: Fraternal or Siamese Twins? A Preliminary Genealogy of Our Twin Fields." *Comparative Education Review* 38 (November): 449–486.

Wolhuter, Charl, Nikolay Popov, Bruno Leutwyler, and Klara Skubic Ermenc. 2013. *Comparative Education at Universities Worldwide*. Sofia: Bulgarian Comparative Education Society and University of Ljubljana Faculty of Arts.

Revisiting comparative education in Latin America: traditions, uses, and perspectives

Felicitas Acosta and Guillermo Ramón Ruiz

ABSTRACT

Comparative education is a field with a tradition that dates back to the beginning of the nineteenth century. The field has come a long way since the times when travellers sought educational experiences that could be applied in their places of origin; it has expanded across the world, though the rhythm of knowledge production varies significantly from one region to the next. More recently, the increased attention to educational internationalisation has enlarged the pool of perspectives linked to the field. In this paper, we examine some of the more recent debates on comparative education to provide an analysis of the field within a specific context: Latin America. From a historical perspective, we analyse the continuity of, and ruptures between, the field on both global and regional fronts. We emphasise specific features of the region: how was comparison introduced, which were the main loci of production and circulation, who tends to use it at present and for what purpose. We focus on the circulation of themes and practices in three periods of time among Latin American countries. A particular form of academic institutionalisation – not driven by universities – is a unique feature of the region that differs from paradigmatic comparative education.

Introduction

Comparative education dates back to the early nineteenth century. Much has changed since the times when travellers set off in search of educational experiences to transfer to their homes countries. While the field today, with its specialised conferences and journals, is studied the world over, the rhythm of intellectual production varies considerably from region to region.

This article will look at both historical and recent discussions in comparative education to analyse the development of the field in Latin America. We will focus on how comparative education developed in a diverse region and, more specifically, on the relationship between comparison and the development of educational policies.

Latin America does not have a continuous or robust tradition of comparative education as an academic field (see Acosta 2011; Acosta and Perez Centeno 2011; Acosta and Ruiz 2015). While some countries in the region, especially those in the Southern Cone, did participate in what is called the 'foreigner pedagogy' when they set up their educational systems (Acosta 2011), the field did not take root or flourish as a consistent academic study (López Velarde 2000). For this reason, and others, an array of international educational agencies have intervened in the region's educational systems, specifically in their implementation, development, and reforms.

Regardless, in analysing educational development, it is possible to distinguish in the region different ways in which comparative education has been used and circulated. We argue that there are *waves of circulation* in the region's different countries, some of them more geared to comparative education as a field and others more closely linked to different uses of comparison. Similarly, there are continuities and ruptures in those waves from the end of the nineteenth century to the beginning of the twenty-first century – the period which witnessed the flourishing of comparative education. These continuities and ruptures can be linked to the ways that the region's educational systems have expanded.

This article is structured in two parts. In the first, principal international trends in the development of comparative education are summarised and applied to the state of the field in Latin America. The second part examines three particular ways that comparison in education has been used in the region: comparative education as individual practice; educational comparison and planning as government practice; and comparison in the practice of international organisations operating in the region. Finally, we present a series of conclusions regarding the field along with reflections on its future development.

Comparative education: international tendencies and their development in Latin America

Significantly, comparative education emerged during a period when nation states were the principal actors in devising educational ideas and practices. The idea of the transfer of practices as well as their use in policies, that is, in the organisation of educational systems, lies at the very origin of comparative education. Early comparative education revolved around at least four major concerns, all of them tied to the problem of transfer: (1) schooling as practice transferable from one context to another; (2) the comparative method as scientific validation of those possible transfers; (3) the tension between that transfer and specific social-cultural contexts; and (4) the transfer of knowledge produced by comparison to educational policy.

As we have pointed out in previous works (Acosta and Pérez Centeno 2011; Acosta 2011; Acosta and Ruiz 2015), comparative education as a field experienced at least five distinct moments as it became institutionalised. The first moment – one completely lacking in structure – consisted of pedagogues or agents of the government travelling to more advanced countries in search of understanding educational experiences that could perhaps be applied in their home countries.

The second moment – one foundational to the field as such – began with the work of Marc-Antoine Jullien de Paris (1775–1848). He ventured a proto-positivist reformulation of educational doctrines, as well as basing the development of educational theory on methodical investigation. This is a case of the transfer of educational ideas and practices based on the collection of international data.

The early twentieth century witnessed the third moment when comparative education was founded as an academic field with the creation of university departments. A period of intense circulation of ideas between thinkers in Europe, especially in England and Germany, centred on the United States, where the first university programmes and research centres in comparative education were created (see Pereyra and 2000). By this point, comparative research was not limited to identifying similarities and differences in educational systems, but took into account the analysis of broader social contexts.

The fourth moment – in the mid-twentieth century – consisted of the consolidation of comparative education as scientific field. This process saw the introduction of quasi-experimental models based on the principle of causality. This new phase was furthered by international organisations which influenced the new agendas in educational policies. The transfer of approaches intensified; the specificities of the previous period blurred, and the relationship between comparative education and educational policy formalised.

The 1990s witnessed further changes in comparative education. This fifth moment responded to the challenges posed by new global socio-economic organisations. It noted the failings of the positivist scientific models in the face of new realities: globalisation represented a breaking point in the conceptual development of the field. Much of the field's intellectual production began to focus on the problem of interconnections, which made for major revisions, reformulations, and conceptual advances. It has been argued that the societies of reference in this new phase are constructed from the standpoint of a global context of comparison; attention should be paid to a new type of global comparison, one that takes into account the transnational changes in policies and politics (Novoa and Yariv-Mashal 2003; Lingard and Rawolle 2009; Steiner-Khamsi 2015). One of the field's central concerns – transfer – is also undergoing a process of re-conceptualisation: transfer, it is argued, must not be seen as linear or unidirectional, but rather as circular and, in some ways, reciprocal (see Steiner-Khamsi and Waldow 2012).

As noted above, Latin America does not have a continuous or robust tradition in the academic field of comparative education. Indeed, it is difficult to conceptualise the region as a whole, not only in relation to comparative education, but also to overall social development: the region is diverse, with an array of geographies and climates, social and cultural groups. That diversity is reflected in the countries' varied social structures, distributions of wealth, customs, and languages. Notwithstanding this diversity, the region does have common heritages, histories, and problems, and faces similar or analogous challenges in both politics and the development of social institutions.

One element of that common heritage is the development of educational systems and the introduction of comparative education in the region. After the wars of independence, the new nation states began to take charge of primary education; according to the notion of common education, the state was envisioned as a teacher state. Through social and cultural homogenisation, Latin American educational systems contributed to national integration and to the development of citizenship.

At this point, the first and second moments in the development of comparative education as a field converge. In configuring their educational systems, some countries in the region, particularly ones in the Southern Cone, played an active role in 'foreigner pedagogy'. As López Velarde (2000) points out, there were cases in the nineteenth century of government officials travelling abroad in search of educational practices to transfer back home: José Luis Mora in Mexico, Andrés Bello in Venezuela and Chile, Domingo Faustino Sarmiento in Argentina and Chile, and José Pedro Varela in Uruguay. Some of those educators participated in early attempts at the scientific organisation of comparative education. Sarmiento, for instance, edited *El Monitor de la Educación Común*, an Argentinean public journal on education that always opened with data, tables, and accounts of educational experiences beyond the region (Acosta 2011).[1]

In Latin American countries, unlike countries that modernised early on, the link between educational systems and economic development was weak through the 1950s at the very least; expansion towards outlying regions was riddled with disparity. Developmentalist policies, some under authoritarian regimes, consolidated the educational systems in some countries and considerably expanded them in others. The process was akin to the massification of educational systems in the developed world; nevertheless, educational supply in the region continued to be unevenly distributed (OREALC UNESCO 1992). In 1960 the net rate of school enrolment in Latin America for children aged 6–11 was 57.7%; by 1980 it had reached 82.4%. For children aged 12–17, in 1960 the rate was 36.3%; by 1980 that had reached 62.6%. This data shows the expansion of primary education coupled with ongoing debates in relation to access to and completion of secondary school.

This partial and unequal expansion of educational systems in the region is related to how comparative education developed. There are no parallels with later moments in the development of the field: academic institutionalisation was scarce, and the introduction of scientific comparison was largely the result of national and international organisations' involvement in the planning of education. As we will see in the next section, the institutionalisation of comparative education is bound to the moment when educational systems in the region were expanding. By the 1960s it was understood that comprehensive planning was necessary to furthering the objective of expansion. Comparison, then, was more closely tied to ways of producing knowledge on educational systems for the sake of diagnoses and of calculation of the resources necessary for its expansion (Latapí 1970; Ruiz 2007).

Since the 1990s repeated structural reforms of Latin American educational systems failed to take into account that the systems are not homogeneous. Even when the reform programmes were similar, they yielded diverse and disparate results. These reforms aimed to extend schooling, and modified different aspects of the educational systems, such as curriculum development; vocational programmes; the evaluation of different educational levels; teacher-education programmes; and university education. During the 1990s, states were pressured by international organisations like the World Bank (WB) and the Inter-American Development Bank (IDB) to implement structural reforms to their educational systems, as part of neoliberal reforms in public spending. The circulation and interconnection of educational policies transfer – central concerns of contemporary comparative education – were topics introduced in this context (see, for example, Beech 2011).[2]

In this section, we presented five moments in the development of comparative education as a field. We also provided an overview of the situation in Latin America, highlighting the relationship between how its educational systems and comparative education developed. In the following section, we will present three waves of circulation in the use of comparison in the region.

Circulation of comparison and education in Latin America

The first section looked at the limitations of the moments in comparative education in ana-lysing regional situations. This section delves more deeply into three particular ways – which we call waves – that comparison in education was deployed in the region. We will discuss comparative education as individual practice; educational comparison and planning as government practice; and comparison in the practice of international organ-isations operating in the region.

Comparative education as individual practice

This wave in the circulation of comparison began in the late nineteenth century and encompassed most of the twentieth century. Two groups of actors were active in this stage of comparative education in Latin America: travelling pedagogues or government agents, and academics. Despite different environments and periods, they had one thing in common: the low level of institutionalisation in their practices.

We have mentioned above the various travellers and the government agents from the region who studied foreign experiences; individuals like José Luis Mora in Mexico, Andrés Bello in Venezuela and Chile, Domingo Faustino Sarmiento in Argentina and Chile, and José Pedro Varela in Uruguay. These figures made comparisons by describing their experi-ences in public reports.

One example is *Educación popular* (*Popular Education*), the book that Domingo Faustino Sarmiento (1834–1888) wrote travelling in Europe and North America in 1849, at the behest of the Chilean government. Sarmiento visited Spain, France, Italy, Germany, England, Canada, and the United States; he was particularly impressed by the educational systems he found in Boston and New York. His report had a significant impact on the Chilean educational debates of the time and foretold the Argentinean debate over the 1884 Act of Common Education (1420 Act), which established free and compulsory primary education (Tedesco and Zacarías 2011).

For the purposes of our argument, two characteristics of the text stand out: first, the detailed nature of the account with its observations *in situ*, and data from primary sources; second, Sarmiento's use of the text to put forth his own educational ideal. Indeed, Sarmiento had requested to make the journey to 'avoid the difficulties and uncer-tainties likely to be produced in putting into practice theoretical knowledge, the only knowledge in existence at the time for carrying out the functions of the principal of a Normal School … ' (Sarmiento 1849/2011, 37; translation ours); after the journey he came up with guidelines for setting up a school system. Although it could be argued that this use of comparison was an institutional practice of the state, the fact is that many of the missions were promoted by the travellers themselves and the influence of their reports was linked to their publication as books.

Academics at universities were the second group of actors in this first wave of the circulation of comparison; they arose in the twentieth century. Comparative education had yet to be established on a wide scale as a topic in teacher-training programmes or universities. This low level of institutionalisation meant little theoretical output; com-parative education and its development were left to a few authors whose publications tended to become reference books. This was true throughout the twentieth century.

López Velarde (2000) could identify only three works on comparative education published between 1940 and 1960: books by Cuban Ema Pérez, by Brazilian Lorenzo Filho, and by Mexican J. Manuel Villalpando. The work by Argentinean Diego Márquez, published in the 1970s, is considered a landmark. Argentinean Gustavo Cirigliano did a study of the state of analysis in comparative education, but that project was undertaken for UNESCO.

This lack of local development is perhaps due to the fact that advances in comparative education at European and North American universities in the 1950s were largely unconnected to the region's context. The work produced at major centres of comparative education, along with their various theoretical and methodological approaches, had little to say about the realities in the Latin American countries, still dealing with the extension of primary education (López Velarde 2000).

The economic and political crises of the 1970s and 1980s, in the framework of the international dissemination of education promoted by international organisations (chiefly UNESCO), brought a de-localisation of research in comparative education in underdeveloped countries (Monfredini 2011). Significant in this context are the reflections yielded by the Fifth World Congress of Comparative Education Societies, held in Paris from July 2 to 6, 1984. Though the theme of the event was 'Dependence and Interdependence in Education: The Role of Comparative Education', in reference to dependency theory – a concept of Latin American origin – there were almost no participants from the region. *Prospects*, the UNESCO's journal, published a special issue on the congress. The Latin American voices in that publication were Velloso from Brazil and Olivera Lahore, an Argentinean based in Costa Rica. Critical of the notion of dependency, the former warned against uncritical acceptance of so-called international cooperation (Velloso 1985), while the latter relativised the very idea of dependency, situating it on the analytical plane of cultural influences (Olivera 1985).

Similarly, production from the 1980s failed to integrate the region into the practices and debates in comparative education. There were, of course, exceptions, like the work of Brazilian thinker Ciavatta Franco and (1992), which used dependency theories, and of Arenas de Sanjuán (1984), which was tied to theories being developed in Spain at the time – classical approaches to comparative education produced by ageing department heads – developed at remaining university *cátedras*. Similarly, by the end of the decade, there were early works by professors at the University of Buenos Aires, Argentina, though their focus was on comparative studies in higher education.

Mexico was the locus of the most intense institutional activity in the 1970s and 1980s, which can be explained by, among other things, the creation of the Center of Educational Studies where Pablo Latapí (1967, 1970) published works in comparative and international education; the publication in Mexico of the *Latin American Review of Educational Studies*, with contributions from Paulston (1971), Carnoy (1971), and Brazilian thinker Gouveia (1971); the annual meeting of the Comparative and International Education Society (CIES) which took place in that country in 1978; and the First Latin American Forum of Comparative Education held at the University of Colima in 1980. In any case, the limited exchange between researchers and the absence of long-standing national academic societies in the field is, indisputably, the most striking feature.[3]

Educational comparison and planning as government practice

Starting in the 1950s, international consensus emerged on the need for detailed planning to give direction to educational policies in regions like Latin America. An attempt was made to modernise the state's administrative structures; planning became one of the methodologies central to achieving efficiency in the administration of public policies as well as the modernisation of the state. It was believed that planning would permit rational and precise allocation of resources and any necessary structural changes. Education, in turn, was envisaged as capable of effecting social and economic development.

Integral planning of education meant formulating and implementing an educational policy by means of a programmed administration (Romero Lozano 1965). The principal theoretical assumptions underlying integral planning in education were (Windham 1975):

- The economic system depended on the educational system insofar as it provided the educated and skilled workforce necessary to economic development. In view of this posited relationship between education and employment, not every kind of training was useful for economic growth.
- The need to accurately forecast increases in the demand for a well-trained workforce (in the formal education system) on the basis of future occupational changes; the assumption was that future changes in the relationship between employment and economic growth could be calculated.

This regional circulation of these new approaches to educational planning across the region brought about the creation of government planning offices, some of them dedicated solely to education, with others geared to broader national economic planning. Early on, the efforts of these planning offices were mostly aimed at the systematisation and analysis of educational statistics and at diagnosing educational systems; there was not much actual planning. Later on, however, studies dedicated not only to diagnosis, but also to educational policy design, were carried out. In this context, the Economic Commission for Latin America and the Caribbean (CEPAL) and the UNESCO created an Educational Planning Division in the Latin American and Caribbean Institute for Economic and Social Planning (ILPES), an organisation directed by Simón Romero Lozano.[4] The regional programmes and seminars given by ILPES and UNESCO constituted essential instruments for the consolidation and communication of educational planning.

Neither the meaning nor the scope of integral planning was defined in conceptual or empirical terms. Important questions were not duly formulated, questions like: What does planning mean? Does it encompass the whole system or just one educational level? Regardless, educational planning agencies proliferated throughout the region as practically every country created educational planning offices. Parallel, rather than coordinated, structures for educational planning were established at the ministerial and national levels.

The studies carried out by these offices served, nonetheless, to show how schooling was actually functioning: What was the school dropout rate? How many graduates were there at every level and in every region? How many students repeated grades? Data important to measuring performance was thus obtained. To carry out and assess these studies, educational statistics were required. Both governments and the population now had access to detailed information on the state of education on the national, regional, and local levels. The comparison of socio-educational descriptions and analysis undoubtedly took place in these institutional environments, though that did not necessarily lead to scientific research of the sort carried out at the time in other contexts like the United States and Europe.

By the mid-1960s, these offices had gained technical expertise and administrative efficiency – thanks, in part, to international and regional seminars and conferences in which government agents participated. Integral education planning led to the publication of planning-books that were global in nature, books that encompassed every area and section of formal education. The aim was to transform education as a whole, which meant that the texts were overly general. The publications were envisioned as reference books for educational policies and their implementation over time. The plans revolved around fixed points of reference that failed to take into account changing conditions or to allow for innovation – a limitation now recognised as significant. Analysis of these documents evidences the lack of inner coherence in many of the region's educational plans. Plan-books did not align overall objectives and specific projects, which has led to the conclusion that the books were not a coherent whole (Ruiz 2007).

These plans failed in almost every country: the objectives were never met, and changing circumstances and contextual problems – neither of which were duly taken into account – had a negative effect on their ability to forecast. Overly rigid, the plans could not adjust to sudden changes in countries characterised by political and economic instability. One UNESCO document, released in 1974, argued that the application of governmental educational plans in Latin America was merely formal; the plans had not served to aid decision-making, they were merely technical documents that offered a general diagnosis of the state of education in a country (OREALC 1974).

Comparative education as a field of knowledge was totally absent in the entire regional circulation of the approach to integral educational planning. Due to the field's weak academic development, it did not have the impact foreseen by theorists like, for example, the Spaniard Pedro Roselló; in the early 1960s he had spoken of a dynamic comparative education capable of inducing or anticipating future scenarios in education (Márquez 1972). Though related to comparative education as *scientific* field and to its methods, this wave of regional circulation was not informed by the academic field of comparative education. The integral planning approach instead made use of statistical comparison: in a context of weak educational development, governments, along with international organisations, imposed the systematic use of educational quantification and statistical models to guide educational policies according to the formula of integral planning.

Comparison in the practice of international organisations in the region

The 1980s witnessed regional economic crises along with the return to democracy in many countries. Educational systems were reformed and redefined; they were diagnosed as a sector in crisis, where the need for international intervention was re-examined. A new period of circulation of comparison began, principally in the context of educational reforms. Studies yielded comparative data that informed decision-making processes as well as reforms aimed at resolving the educational crisis. In the framework of structural adjustment and of austerity programmes in social policy, international financial organisations pressured governments to cut funding for educational programmes.

Latin American countries were affected by the recommendations on education made by the Organisation of American States; UNESCO (through its regional office based in Chile, the Regional Bureau of Education for Latin America and the Caribbean – OREALC); the Organisation of Ibero-American States (OEI); CEPAL; the WB; the IDB; and the Organisation for Economic Co-operation and Development (OECD). While some organisations acted mainly as agencies of technical cooperation (UNESCO and OEI), others acted as funding bodies (the WB and the IDB). The intervention of all of these entities in technical cooperation made themselves felt increasingly through reports and sectorial, national, and regional documents. In the area of education, these international organisations deployed a twofold strategy: (1) as a pillar of social policy, and (2) as part of economic policy geared to improving productivity.

The international studies produced by both these types of organisations made increasing use of comparison over the course of a period when reforms deepened. The region's educational systems, their expansion, and range were compared, as were educational results (graduate rates, years of schooling, dropout indicators, and so forth). Systems were ranked, in effect, in terms of quality, mainly at the university level.

Starting in the late twentieth century, particularly in the last decade, organisations like the OEI, the International Institute for Educational Planning (IIEP UNESCO) – through its regional seat in Buenos Aires created in 1998 – the Program of Promotion of Educational Reform in Latin America, and the Caribbean-PREAL and the CEPAL, geared their efforts towards regional comparison and the development of case studies. IIEP UNESCO Buenos Aires in alliance with OEI created the Information System for Educational Trends in Latin America (SITEAL), which was specifically aimed at producing comparative information on Latin American educational systems.

Indeed, the documents produced by these organisations in the last 10 years show that the agencies geared to regional integration, and to disseminating knowledge and research in education, make use of comparison fluctuating between case studies and regional comparison. The themes of the documents are largely the same, mostly concerns arose during the era of reform mentioned above (ICT, evaluation of quality and exclusion in education, of the teaching and learning processes, of school culture and higher education – particularly in relation to teacher accreditation and education); the approach is qualitatively oriented.[5]

By contrast, the organisations that generate regional data and indicators are more quantitative in their approach. SITEAL[6] and CEPAL,[7] to name just two, look to statistical publications and make use of diverse indicators tackled from national and regional perspectives. A number of CEPAL's publications are based on analysis of so-called successful cases.[8]

Two elements stand out in these comparisons: the weight of the regional dimension in the comparison of educational indicators in the region's different countries; which experiments are considered successful, and used as the basis for 'good practices' or cited as 'lessons learned' for Latin American countries. PREAL reports are especially prone to speaking in terms of 'good practices'.

While this third wave in the use of comparison is not centred on universities or other academic environments, it does engage in the transfers of policies, a core dimension of international scholarship on comparative education. The use of comparison in terms of 'lessons learned' does not mean that transfer is problematised – quite the opposite.

Indeed, this would be the case in producing *comparative information for the development of educational policies*: information made more robust by the use of qualitative as well as quantitative methods but closer to a comparative educative of solutions (Cowen 2017).

Towards a new wave of circulation?

At present, participation in comparative education in Latin America continues to be largely individual, though more nuanced, by the creation and extension of national comparative education societies in the last decade, which sometimes serve as an institutional platform for university academics. Five national comparative education societies were formed or re-established at the beginning of the twenty-first century: Venezuela (2000), Argentina (2001), Mexico (2003), and Uruguay (2009). In 2014, the *Sociedad Iberoamericana de Educación Comparada* was founded comprising several national societies in Latin America, along with the Spanish and the Portuguese societies of comparative education. The world congresses organised by the World Council of Comparative Education Societies (WCCES) in Brazil (1987), Cuba (2004), and Argentina (2013) may have catalysed the formation of new national scholarly societies in comparative education in the region.[9] Furthermore, the next World Congress of Comparative Education Societies will take place in Mexico in 2019.

Compilations and journals have been published by these national societies. For example, the Mexican Society for Comparative Education has in recent years published a group of books on comparative education in Latin America, as well as on internationalisation and regional comparison. Similarly, the Argentinean Society of Comparative Studies in Education (SAECE) established in 2010 the *Latin American Review of Comparative Education* (*Revista Latinoamericana de Educación Comparada*, RELEC). Thus far, 10 issues of the review with some 75 articles have been published. A look at the articles published in this journal shows that 15% focus on theoretical–methodological problems in the field of comparative education, whilst 31% are related primarily to the international comparison, and 19.4% deal with globalisation and internationalisation in education (Acosta and Ruiz 2016).

Nevertheless, this new manifestation of comparative education's 'way of being' in Latin America bears similarities with the previous waves. First, it is a particular – non-traditional – form of academic institutionalisation, insofar as it is not developed at universities – this indeed could be a unique feature of Latin America that differs from paradigmatic comparative education. Second, it is linked to the agenda of educational policy. Indeed, at the last five biennial meetings of the SAECE, 30% of papers presented addressed policy issues while 18% dealt with educational reform (Acosta 2016). The articles published in the RELEC reflect the same tendency: 41% of the contents of the first nine issues deal with policy, and 24% with inclusion in the educational system (Acosta 2016). At this point, we can ask if we are already in the presence of a fourth and new wave of circulation of comparison in Latin America.

Conclusion

In this article, we analysed the development of comparative education in Latin America. We compared how the field of comparative education was structured between countries that modernised early and in Latin American countries. Common elements include the notion of transfer in the configuration of the educational systems, foreign journeys as a means to produce knowledge, and the comparison of data to develop educational policies. The relative weakness of comparative education as academic field explains in part the differences in its development in the region versus other parts of the world. In this framework, and in an attempt to conceptualise other forms of comparative education, we suggested that educational comparison has, in the Latin American region, a specific 'way of being'; one characterised by distinct waves of circulation tied to educational policies aimed at the extension of compulsory schooling.

The first wave entailed individual practices of comparison, mainly travellers in the nineteenth and early twentieth century. Those practices were more enmeshed in the development of comparative education as a field. We call them 'individual practices' because of their low level of institutionalisation.

The second wave encompassed the rise of educational planning in Latin America in the mid-twentieth century and the need to further expand educational systems. What was at stake in this wave was not comparative education per se, but rather the appropriation of tools of comparison by national and international organisations (planning agencies). A link can be found here to what some authors consider as the moment of consolidation of comparative education as scientific field due to the use of quantitative methods in the study of educational development.

The third wave ensued in the late twentieth century, when reforms in the Latin American educational systems were enacted at the insistence of international finance organisations while others provided technical assistance in conjunction with local education ministries. Though comparative education was not academic in nature during this wave either, it was different from the previous wave in several senses: first, comparative information was produced, during this third wave, to guide policies to *extend and reform* educational systems; second, the scope for comparison was regional – within Latin America – rather than local/national; third, the methodology during this wave included qualitative, not only quantitative, studies. Producing comparative information, developing 'good practices', and heeding 'lessons learned' were privileged practices in the line of a comparative education of solutions (Cowen 2017).

We can assert that the first wave – comparative education as an individual practice – anticipated a later tendency mentioned above: academics grouped in national associations of comparative education, which could be a new way of regional circulation of comparison. Pertinent as well, of course, will be the contents of other congresses and meetings and of the publications of other associations throughout the region. The field of comparative education entails multiple irregular flows: as Cowen puts it, 'There are no rules of morphology'. Meanwhile, questions are raised about the future direction of this new manifestation of comparative education in Latin America: it has yet to be determined if it is geared to 'questions of governance or is, rather, part of the historical journey that is comparative education' (Cowen 2017).

Notes

1. *El Monitor de la Educación Común* was a publication edited by the National Education Council from 1881 to 1976 with some interruptions during the fifties (1949–1959) and during the

sixties (1961–1966) due to political issues. As from the first number of the journal it included articles which developed the comparison of class days with countries such as the United States; the proposals of feminising the teaching profession in countries such as France and Prussia; reports of an inspector on comparative data between the United States, Buenos Aires, and Chile (Year I, N. 2); examples of 'fines and legal penalties imposed by law on educational functionaries, taken from the education laws of New York' (Year I, N. 3). Furthermore, a project of resolution is proposed in journal number 7:

> … Point III, Art. 7: There will be created in the Capital a Magazine of Public Instruction under the direction of the Director General. This magazine will be composed of four principal sections: 1 Original works referring to education in the Republic; 2 Transcriptions or translations of works by foreign educationalists; 3 Review of foreign educational movements; 4 Official documents. (Year I, N. 7, 1882)

2. In Latin America, structural adjustments were defined by the WB, the International Monetary Fund, and other financial organisations. They implied a set of programs of stabilisation and adjustment, which involve the reduction of state spending, the devaluation of currencies to promote exports, the increase of public and private savings and a significant reduction in the state sector. These programs sought to liberalise international exchange and eliminate protectionism. Oreja Cerruti and Vior (2016) also point out that, since the mid-twentieth century, the role of international organisations in setting public policy in Latin America has grown. That influence takes the shape of communicating policy approaches and creating consensus on them; setting goals and national commitments towards meeting them; and policy funding and restrictions based on performance. In education, international funding organisations, along with the Economic Commission for Latin America and the Caribbean (CEPAL) and the United Nations Educational, Scientific and Cultural Organisation (UNESCO) and the Program for the Promotion of Educational Reform in Latin American and the Caribbean (PREAL), have backed the reforms in the region's educational systems—which varied from country to country according to history and specific traits – implemented starting in the 1990s.

3. There were several national societies in Latin America in the 1970–1990 period (e.g. Argentina, Brazil, Colombia, and Cuba), but were short-lived: Argentina (1970s); Colombia (1980s). See Masemann, Bray, and Manzon (2007).

4. Another institution equally important for its impact on educational policies, although only in Brazil, was the Brazilian Center for Analysis and Planning (CEBRAP).

5. For the case of the IIEP, see: 'Los sistemas nacionales de inspección y/o supervisión escolar. Revisión de la literatura y análisis de casos', 'La educación secundaria en foco: análisis de políticas de inclusión en Argentina, Canadá, Chile y España', 'El desarrollo profesional docente centrado en la escuela. Concepciones, políticas y experiencias'. These are available at: http://www.iipe-buenosaires.org.ar/documentos. For the OEI, see the special issues of the last five years, with respect to the educational programs involving technology in the classrooms or the evaluation of education, where the kind of comparison oscillates between regional and national comparison, and case studies. They are available at: http://www.rieoei.org/rie_contenedor.php?numero=rie56, and http://www.rieoei.org/rie53.htm, respectively. With respect to other problems, such as childhood in school or the learning of curricular areas (such as mathematics or reading), the case studies seem to be those with the highest degree of incidence when dealing with these issues. They are, respectively, available at: http://www.rieoei.org/rie43.htm, http://www.rieoei.org/rie46.htm.

6. The SITEAL, due to its goal, produces documents based on quantitative information, and generates a database with standardised indicators which arise from national census in the countries of Latin America and links to other sources of information. The 'Atlas of educational inequalities in Latin America' analyses the territorial dispositions of the social and economic phenomena of the region, the 'SITEAL database', the 'Statistical Summaries' the 'Notebooks' (such as 'Configuraciones espaciales de escenarios urbanos y rurales. Desafíos pendientes en los procesos de inclusión educativa', to take only some examples) point in this direction.

7. Examples of this are publications such as 'Aporte del sistema educativo a la reducción de las brechas digitales. Una mirada desde las mediciones PISA', 'Trabajo, educación y salud de las niñas en América Latina y el Caribe: indicadores elaborados en el marco de la plataforma de Beijing', their 'Anuarios estadísticos de América Latina y el Caribe'. Available at: http://www.eclac.org/publicaciones/search.asp?desDoc=Educaci%F3n&functioninput=Educaci%F3n&cat=37&tipDoc=&pais=&idioma=&agno=.
8. For example: 'La incorporación de tecnologías digitales en educación. Modelos de identificación de buenas prácticas', 'Las políticas de tecnología para escuelas en América Latina y el mundo: visiones y lecciones'. Available at: http://www.eclac.org/publicaciones/search.asp?desDoc=Educaci%F3n&functioninput=Educaci%F3n&cat=37&tipDoc=&pais=&idioma=&agno=.
9. Similar processes are discussed in Manzon (2011), and Masemann, Bray, and Manzon (2007).

Disclosure statement

No potential conflict of interest was reported by the authors.

References

Acosta, F. 2011. "La educación comparada en América Latina: estado de situación y prospectiva." *Revista Latinoamericana de Educación Comparada* 2: 73–83.
Acosta, F. 2016. "*Comparative Education in Latin America: Between Traditions and Uses. An Overview.*" Paper Presented at *XVI WCCES Congress*, Beijing, August 22–26.
Acosta, F., and C. G. Pérez Centeno. 2011. "Re-bordering Comparative Education in Latin America: Between Global Limits and Local Characteristics." *International Review of Education* 57 (3–4): 477–496.
Acosta, F., and G. Ruiz. 2015. "Estudio introductorio." In *Repensando la Educación Comparada. Lecturas desde Iberoamérica. Entre los viajeros del siglo XIX y la globalización*, edited by G. Ruiz and F. Acosta, 15–26. Barcelona: Octaedro.
Acosta, F., and G. Ruiz. 2016. "Los primeros 10 números de RELEC: un momento para el cambio." *Revista Latinoamericana de Educación Comparada* 10: 8–10.
Arenas de Sanjuán, C., et al. 1984. *Investigación en educación comparada*. San Luis: UNSL.

Beech, J. 2011. "Continuidades y cambios en el campo educativo global. Influencias externas en la formación docente en Argentina y Brasil." In *Internacionalización. Políticas educativas y reflexión pedagógica en un medio global*, edited by M. Caruso and H. Tenorth, 183–214. Buenos Aires: Granica.

Carnoy, M. 1971. "Un enfoque de sistemas para evaluar la educación: ilustrado con datos de Puerto Rico." *Revista del Centro de Estudios Educativos* 1 (3): 9–49.

Ciavatta Franco, M. 1992. "Estudios comparados en educación en América Latina. Una discusión teórico-metodológica a partir de la cuestión del otro." In *Estudios comparados en educación en América Latina*, edited by A. Puiggrós, G. Bertussi, and M. CiavattaFranco, 11–30. Buenos Aires: Libros del Quirquincho.

Cowen, R. 2017. "Narrating and Relating Educational Reform and Comparative Education." In *Critical Analyses of Educational Reforms in an Era of Transnational Governance*, edited by E. Hultqvist, S. Lindblad, and T. Popkewitz, 23–39. Dordrecht: Springer.

Gouveia, A. J. 1971. "La investigación educacional en Brasil." *Revista del Centro de Estudios Educativos* 1 (4): 64–96.

Latapí, P. 1967. *La enseñanza superior en Centroamérica*. México: Centro de Estudios Educativos.

Latapí, P. 1970. *Educación y sistemas escolares en América Latina: problemática y tendencias de solución*. México: Centro de Estudios Educativos.

Lingard, B., and S. Rawolle. 2009. "Rescaling and Reconstituting Education Policy: The Knowledge Economy and the Scalar of Global Fields." In *Re-reading Education Policies: Studying the Policy Agenda of the Twenty-First Century*, edited by M. Simons, M. Olsen, and M. Peters, 1–15. Rotterdam: Sense.

López Velarde, J. 2000. *Historia reciente de los estudios de Educación Comparada en Hispanoamérica con referencia a la educación de adultos*. México: CREFAL.

Manzon, M. 2011. *Comparative Education: The Construction of a Field*. Dordrecht: Springer.

Márquez, A. D. 1972. *Educación comparada. Teoría y método*. Buenos Aires: El Ateneo.

Masemann, V., M. Bray, and M. Manzon. 2007. *Common Interests, Uncommon Goals: Histories of the World Council of Comparative Education Societies and Its Members*. Dordrecht: Springer.

Monfredini, I. 2011. "Políticas de ensino superior, ciência e tecnologia e as condições produção intelectual no Brasil: uma perspectiva comparada com Argentina e México." Paper presented at the *IV Congreso Nacional y III Encuentro Internacional de Estudios Comparados en Educación*, Buenos Aires, June 16–17.

Novoa, A., and T. Yariv-Mashal. 2003. "Comparative Research in Education: A Mode of Governance or a Historical Journey?" *Comparative Education* 39 (4): 423–438.

Oficina Regional de Educación de la UNESCO-OREALC. 1974. *Algunas observaciones sobre la planificación de la educación en América Latina*. Santiago de Chile: UNESCO.

Oficina Regional de Educación de la UNESCO-OREALC. 1992. *Situación educativa de América Latina y el Caribe 1980-1989*. Santiago de Chile: UNESCO.

Olivera, C. E. 1985. "Is Education in Latina America Dependent?" *Prospects* 15 (2): 227–238.

Oreja Cerruti, B., and S. Vior. 2016. "Education and the international credit organisations. Loans and Recommendations to America Latina (2000-2015)." *Journal of Supranational Policies of Education* 4: 18–37.

Paulston, R. 1971. "Innovación y cambio en la educación superior peruana." *Revista del Centro de Estudios Educativos* 1 (2): 29–42.

Pereyra, M. 2000. "La construcción de la educación comparada como disciplina académica. Defensa e ilustración de la historia de las disciplinas." In *Teoría y desarrollo de la investigación en educación comparada*, edited by J. Calderón LópezVelarde, 27–80. México: Plaza y Valdés.

Romero Lozano, S. 1965. *El planeamiento de la educación. Aspectos conceptuales y metodológicos*. La Plata: Ministerio de Educación de la provincia de Buenos Aires.

Ruiz, G. 2007. "De la planificación de las políticas educativas a la evaluación de la calidad del sistema educativo. Un análisis desde la perspectiva histórica y comparada de la política educacional en el período 1958-1998." *PhD diss.*, University of Buenos Aires.

Sarmiento, D. F. 1849/2011. "Informe al Ministro de Instrucción Pública." In *Educación Popular*, edited by D. F. Sarmiento, 37–45. Buenos Aires: UNIPE.

Steiner-Khamsi, G. 2015. "La transferencia de políticas como herramienta para comprender la lógica de los sistemas educativos." In *Repensando la Educación Comparada. Lecturas desde Iberoamérica. Entre los viajeros del siglo XIX y la globalización*, edited by G. Ruiz and F. Acosta, 27–40. Barcelona: Octaedro.

Steiner-Khamsi, G., and F. Waldow, eds. 2012. *Policy Borrowing and Lending. World Yearbook of Education 2012*. London: Routledge.

Tedesco, J. C., and I. Zacarías. 2011. "Presentación." In *Educación Popular*, edited by D. F. Sarmiento, 9–26. Buenos Aires: UNIPE.

Velloso, J. 1985. "Dependency and Education: Reproduction or Conspiracy?" *Prospects* 15 (2): 205–212.

Windham, D. 1975. "The Macro-planning of Education: Why It Fails, Why It Survives, and the Alternatives." *Comparative Education Review* 19 (2): 187–201.

Towards a new articulation of comparative educations: cross-culturalising research imaginations

Keita Takayama

ABSTRACT

The Japan Comparative Education Society (JCES) was founded in 1965 with its flagship Japanese-language journal *Hikakukyoikukenkyu* (*Comparative Education Research*) first published in 1975. The organisation currently has around 1000 members, making it the second largest comparative education society in the world. Though JCES members have long engaged in methodological and theoretical debates, their insights are hardly acknowledged in the English-language literature. Drawing on a review of the Japanese-language literature and semi-structured interviews with 25 JCES members, this paper identifies a particular intellectual tradition within JCES, often referred to as the area-studies approach to comparative education. This approach, often practised by JCES researchers specialising in developing countries in Asia, has long constituted the mainstay of comparative education scholarship in Japan. This paper traces the formation of this intellectual tradition, and focuses on its complex relationship with the dominant paradigm of 'paradigmatic' English-language comparative education scholarship. The paper shows how 'other' comparative education societies – such as the JCES – can be looked to as a resource with which to 'provincialise' the way comparative education research is conceptualised in English-language academia, and to cross-culturalise the field of comparative education.

Revisiting comparative educations

The field of comparative education has long recognised diversity in what counts as comparative education. Many comparativists have recognised that the tensions and dynamics generated by different methodological and epistemological orientations are an important source of dialogue and reflection for the field (Cowen 1996, 2000; Epstein 1988; Rust et al. 1999; Manzon 2011). Robert Cowen (1996, 2000) uses the term 'comparative educations' to acknowledge the field's methodological and epistemological plurality, as well as to encourage deeper reflection on the nature of the comparative knowledge we produce. Indeed, the plurality of comparative educations emerged as a result of the field's engagement with a range of topics, phenomena and perspectives: 'nationalism, national character, trends, convergence, dependency, neo-colonialism and specialist sub-literature, such as comparative higher education' (Cowen 2000, 335). A variety of methodologies and ways of conceptualising the world in which education is embedded co-exist in the field, resulting in 'a world of multiple comparative educations'; they not only 'read different worlds' but are also 'in different worlds' (Cowen 2000, 335).

While the insights generated through the recognition of the field's plurality are important, conversation remains constrained by parameters set by select European and North American comparative education research, or what I call after Manzon (2011, 45) 'paradigmatic' comparative education. Even Cowen's important discussion ignores the existence of comparative educations as practised and conceptualised outside Europe and North America. Likewise, Manzon's discussion of comparative education as a social field in the Bourdieuian sense of the term focuses largely on comparative scholars in the Anglo-European societies, though some chapters discuss non-English-language-based comparative education societies. The tendency is to equate the term 'comparative educations' with the divergent research traditions and approaches that have emerged from and been debated within European and North American comparative education.

The global plurality of comparative educations has been more explicitly recognised by those involved in the World Congress of Comparative Education Societies (WCCES), which comprises over 40 regional and national comparative education societies. One such scholar, Mark Bray, has re-articulated Cowen's notion of comparative educations in the broader international context of the WCCES. He has highlighted the different institutional histories and scholarly traditions of comparative education scholarship as practised in different regional and national comparative education societies (see Bray 2002, 2003a, 2003b; Bray and Manzon 2014; Manzon and Bray 2006; Masemann, Bray, and Manzon 2007).

While such recognition of global plurality is important, existing scholarship falls short of addressing two related, critical issues. First, it focuses on institutional histories and traditions of different societies, while paying little attention to the knowledges they produce or how they relate to the hegemonic knowledge produced in paradigmatic comparative education. The celebration of global comparative educations treats different national and regional societies as separate 'containers' within which distinctive histories, traditions and knowledges are generated, thus obscuring transnational flows and interactions of comparative knowledges. Second, this recognition of plurality is disconnected from the unequal power relations that hierarchically position comparative education knowledges produced in different languages and in different parts of the world. As Manzon (2011, 45) points out, there exists in comparative education 'a hierarchical structure in the field of knowledge production, wherein some countries occupy a central "paradigmatic" position for other countries located at the periphery'. That is, comparativists in all parts of the world know the leading theorists based in North American and select European institutions. Yet few comparativists in the paradigmatic societies know any scholarship, let alone theoretical work, produced by non-English-using, non-Western comparativists. What postcolonial historian Dipesh Chakrabarty (2000, 28) calls the problem of 'asymmetric ignorance' has afflicted the field of comparative education since its inception.

Without an explicit acknowledgement of this uneven power structure within the field's knowledge production and distribution, the existing scholarship on the plurality of comparative educations perpetuates a cosmetic form of multiculturalism – incorporation of plurality without questioning the terms of 'inclusion' itself (Chakrabarty 2000; Hokari

2011). The epistemological, methodological and even ontological premises of comparative education research are assumed to be similar – if not identical – around the world, and thus do not warrant serious scrutiny (see Rappleye and Komatsu 2015). This presumption of sameness not only obscures the way in which uneven power relations shape the production and distribution of comparative knowledge both in the paradigmatic centres and peripheries; it prevents us from utilising the fundamental differences as a starting point for a dialogue, or for 'cross-culturalising' research methodology and imagination (Hokari 2011). It is time to go beyond the usual juxtaposition of the diverse institutional histories and intellectual traditions of comparative educations around the world. Instead, we must acknowledge the different knowledges of comparative education that are generated around the world, and use the differences to provincialise the dominant form and content of knowledge produced in, and disseminated from, paradigmatic comparative education.

One step towards such a shift would be to seek methodological and theoretical insights produced in marginalised comparative education societies as an epistemic resource (Takayama, Sriprakash, and Connell 2017). That is, to make a decisive shift in the way we perceive and treat 'other' comparative educations; we start viewing them as epistemic resources. This is a way of pursing what the late historian Minoru Hokari (2011, 254) calls, after Gayatria Spivak, 'unlearning the privilege of knowingness' or what Arjun Appadurai (2000) calls 'epistemological diffidence'. This would mean that comparative education, as practised and conceptualised in Europe and North America, could begin to recognise its own limits and provinciality and open itself up to the possibilities of plural research imaginations. This epistemic shift is fundamental to the reconstruction of comparative education as a dialogic space whereby different epistemological, methodological and ontological premises of comparative education are recognised and utilised for cross-culturalising work (Takayama 2011; Takayama 2015; Takayama, Sriprakash, and Connell 2017).

This paper turns to the Japan Comparative Education Society (JCES hereafter) as an intellectual resource with which to cross-culturalise comparative education. JCES is described as one of the field's 'pioneering societies' and yet one of the least represented in the debate of the 'centre' (Manzon 2011, 78). Founded in 1965, JCES currently has approximately 1000 members, making it one of the largest comparative education societies in the world, second only to North America's Comparative and International Education Society. Its flagship Japanese-language journal *Hikakukyoikukenkyu* (*Comparative Education Research*, hereafter JCER), first published in 1975, has consistently featured methodological and theoretical debates, some of which correspond to similar debates in paradigmatic comparative education (see Sugimura 2011 for a comprehensive review). Their perspectives and insights are only published in Japanese, and as such, are never acknowledged in the English-language 'centre' of comparative education. It is this rather unidirectional flow of intellectual influence, and the epistemic ignorance this creates in the centre, that this paper aims to address.

'Dangerous' comparative education

This paper draws upon the recent postcolonial critique of the political economy of social science knowledge production (see Takayama, Sriprakash, and Connell 2017). In her influential work *Southern Theory*, Raewyn Connell (2007) argues that northern, metropolitan sociologists perpetuate global inequality in knowledge production by treating theories and concepts generated in the particular geographical, temporal and cultural context of Western modernity as 'universal'. Continuing to 'work through categories produced in the metropole' (Northern academic powerhouses such as North America and Western Europe), they fail to enter into 'dialogue with the ideas produced by the colonised world' (Connell 2007, xi). To reverse the epistemic ignorance of modern social thought, which she characterises as 'an ethno-sociology of metropolitan society' (226), Connell (2007) calls for learning from various intellectual traditions in 'other' parts of the world in an attempt to take them seriously – 'as texts to learn from, not just about' (x).

In the discipline of history, Minoru Hokari (2011) develops a similar critical insight in his *Gurindji Journey*. Hokari turns to the historical practice of an indigenous people in Central Australia, the Gurindji people, and highlights the highly localised historical narrative of Gurindji elders that is infused with their 'mythical' creationist worldview. Here, he makes a distinction between local history and localised history, suggesting that the latter is dangerous because of its rejection of the empiricist premise of the discipline of history itself. Hokari redefines the Gurindji elders' storytelling as a form of localised history as opposed to a myth or folklore to be studied anthropologically, and uses its radical alterity to provincialise the universalist epistemology (empiricism) of history as a discipline. Drawing on Chakrabarty (2000), Hokari (2011) argues that to cross-culturalise the discipline of history itself, historians need to 'acknowledge the limits of their (historical disciplines') universality, and seek the possibility of communication with histories which lie beyond these limits' (254). The cross-culturalising work proposed here contrasts with the cosmetic integration of multicultural local histories which invite multicultural agents to be part of the 'good' historical narrative – 'good' in a sense that it conforms to the protocols of the discipline – thus failing to challenge the underpinning epistemology of the discipline of history itself (see Chakrabarty 2000).

Building on these critical perspectives, I conceptualise Japanese comparativists' insights as a valuable intellectual resource to learn from. Here, my intention is not to anthropologise them by tracing the sources of their unique insights to the particular cultural, institutional and historical context of JCES, though admittedly some degree of this is necessary to contextualise their thoughts. More importantly, I intend to deploy a particular intellectual tradition within JCES as a 'dangerous' kind of comparative education. Dangerous not in that it refuses to accept the empiricist premises of comparative education scholarship as suggested by Hokari's notion of localised history, but in that it rejects some of the protocols around legitimate research and knowledge. It is this liminality of JCES that exposes the limits of the universality often attributed to paradigmatic comparative education, as well as that helps us to cross-culturalise comparative education research.

In what follows, I first describe the key epistemological, ontological and methodological premises that characterise comparative education among a particular group of JCES researchers. I identify their critical insights into the form and content of knowledge produced in, and disseminated from, paradigmatic comparative education scholarship. I then use their 'radical difference' as a point of departure to explore different research imaginations than those taken for granted in paradigmatic comparative education.

I must stress here that JCES is not a homogeneous entity in terms of its research orientations and approaches. Indeed, JCES houses multiple – often contested – research orientations, and there exists considerable epistemological and methodological divergence (see Yamada 2011; Yamada and Liu 2011). The area-studies approach to comparative education, the focus of my analysis here, has maintained its dominance in JCES; and yet this has been increasingly challenged by policy-oriented and development-oriented comparativists, many of whom were trained overseas and have now gained a significant presence in JCES (see Kamogawa 2010; Yamada 2011). My subsequent discussion brackets this internal diversity and contestation and focuses on the key theoretical and methodological insights of the area-studies comparativists.[1]

This group of comparativists consider themselves as area-studies (*chiikikenkyu*) specialists who focus on 'developing' countries, primarily in South America and Asia. Many are affiliated with area-studies experts, outside education scholarship circles, who specialise in the same targeted countries and regions. I select this group of JCES scholars not just because they are different from the paradigmatic comparative education research tradition, but because they are also highly critical of it, and as such, are the most 'dangerous' methodologically and epistemologically. My discussion of this group should not be construed as a totalising representation of JCES, nor as an attempt to legitimise its relative dominance in JCES. I use the uniqueness of the JCES's area-studies scholars as a heuristic to cross-culturalise comparative education, and so to rearticulate the notion of comparative educations.

The following discussion of JCES's area-studies approach to comparative education is based on two data sources. First, it is informed by a review of the Japanese-language literature on comparative research methodology produced by JCES members. It draws on every methodological article and special issue published in JCER, as well as every major book on comparative education published in Japanese. Miki Sugimura's (2011) comprehensive review of the methodological debates in JCES was particularly helpful in identifying the relevant articles and books. Second, it draws on interview data with 25 JCES researchers collected between June 2011 and December 2015. Of 25 participants, five clearly represent the JCES's area-studies tradition, while the others are either familiar with, and sympathetic to, the tradition, or highly critical of it. I focus on the data collected from the former, while using the data from the latter as an additional, comparative reference point. All the five area-focused JCES members were trained in the leading Japanese institutions in comparative education and are currently based in Japanese universities, while nearly a half of the second group were trained overseas. The semi-structured interviews focused on their engagement with the comparative education research produced in paradigmatic comparative education; how they locate the North American and European comparative knowledge within their research and teaching activities, including their past graduate school training, and their current graduate student supervision. The interview data were further triangulated with the information retrieved from the review of Japanese-language publications.

The area-studies approach

Underpinning the methodological and epistemological discussion among Japanese comparativists over the last four decades is their sense of marginality in relation to Eurocentric comparative education knowledge production and distribution. As many Japanese comparative scholars acknowledge (e.g. Kobayashi 1975; Otsuka 2005; Umakoshi 1992, 2007), the field is inherently Western in origin. The effort to study foreign education existed in Japan from the early stage of modernisation, and some engaged in systemic comparative analyses as early as in the late nineteenth century (Ishii and Umakoshi 1990; Umakoshi 2007). However, comparative education could not have been established as an academic field in Japan without the 'importation' of the body of knowledge from Europe and North America and the academic legitimisation that came with its Western origins. In the nascent stages of comparative education in Japan, most 'classic' works of Anglo-European comparativists (e.g. Bereday, Hans, Hilker, Jullien, Kandel, Sadler and Schneider) were translated into Japanese (Sugimura 2011, 262). All the Japanese introductory textbooks on comparative education narrate the field's 'foundational' history based on the genealogy of these Western comparativists' classic works (see e.g. Ishizuki 2001, Okihara 1981; Umakoshi 2007; Yoshida 1990).

One of the distinguishing features of JCES is its tendency to situate scholarship within Japanese area studies with a methodological emphasis on fieldwork. Many leading Japanese comparativists stress the importance of fieldwork as the central methodological approach (see Nishino 2011; Otsuka 1994, 2005; Umakoshi 1992, 2007; Yoshida 1990). They assert that an understanding of foreign education demands a comprehensive grasp of its host society and culture. Prolonged immersion in foreign societies, proficiency in local languages and extensive use of written materials in local languages have formed the fundamentals of quality comparative scholarship in JCES (Yamada and Liu 2011).

This area-studies approach, or what Ehara (2001) describes as 'area studies of education' (chiikikyoikukenkyu), was firmly established in JCES by the mid-1990s (Otsuka 1994). This was when JCES's research focus shifted from Western industrial nations, with which Japan had long attempted to 'catch up', to developing countries for which Japan had now become one of the key international donors (Kitamura 2005). The conventional approach to comparative education was criticised for its narrow focus on Western industrial nations, as well as for a lack of empirical and methodological rigour. According to the late Toru Umakoshi (1992), arguably the founding scholar of this area-studies approach, many comparative studies at the time simply summarised government reports and scholarly studies in the targeted nations (mostly advanced Western countries), without engaging in any original data-generating fieldwork (see also Ishii and Umakoshi 1990; Kobayashi 1975; Niibori 1975; Otsuka 1994). Japanese comparativists then recognised that integrating the area-studies approach was a way to renew the field. This would allow for the redefinition of comparative education as 'area studies of education' with a distinctive methodological and epistemological tradition (Chikada 2011; Umakoshi 1992, 2007).[2]

Drawing on Japanese and non-Japanese area-studies scholarship, Umakoshi (1992, 2007) argues that the primary focus of area studies is the description of unique features of a given area, rather than the discovery of 'universal' laws and theories. In his view, the underdevelopment of area-studies methodology – fieldwork – has rendered JCES vulnerable, leading many Japanese comparativists to borrow carelessly or imitate theoretical work imported from paradigmatic comparative education (Umakoshi 1992, 22, 2007, 49). The ethnographic approach is thought to enable comparative researchers to question the ethnocentrism embedded in the 'elitist Western concepts and models' born from social science disciplines.[3] Umakoshi thus regards the in-depth knowledge of targeted areas, generated through a ground-up approach, as a basis for Japanese comparativists' critical engagement with the universalist premises of Western theories; he proposes this to be a distinguishing feature of JCES.[4] Notable here is how Umakoshi positions area-studies' field-work as a basis for subsequent critical theoretical engagements. The constant interaction between fieldwork and theory (*hanpukuundo*) is central to his formulation of the area-studies approach to comparative education research.

However, the primacy of description, or 'fact-finding' drifted away from the next stage of comparative research, theory building and engagement, with subsequent generations of comparativists.[5] Revisiting Umakoshi's formulation, Yutaka Otsuka (2005), the former president of JCES and an expert on Chinese education, sees an exploitative tendency in viewing fieldwork as a tool for theoretical development and refinement. In his view, the practice does not lead to 'the construction of original theory that is unique to the field' (260), as the use of externally generated theoretical tools prevents researchers from devel-oping a thorough understanding and appreciation of what the field presents. As such, Otsuka rejects Umakoshi's formulation as a form of 'weak eclecticism' (260) and instead calls for comparativists to put aside theoretical considerations and to develop their 'intui-tive sensitivities' (*chokusetsuteki kanjusei*) towards the field (262).

The same reservation towards the subordination of fieldwork to theoretical consider-ations has been expressed by other, more contemporary scholars. Setsuo Nishino (2011), a specialist in Islamic education in South East Asia, and whose scholarship is highly praised by Umakoshi (2007, 51), warns:

> We should not blind ourselves to differences by seeing things through dominant ideologies [theories] and generalizing them … Such pressure for generalisation and theorisation has ren-dered comparative education research vulnerable. (135)

Likewise, Morishita, Hattori, and Kamogawa (2013), three area-study comparativists specia-lising in South East Asia and winners of the JCES's prestigious Hiratsuka Award, call for a cautious approach towards theory and theory building in comparative research, in a manner that closely echoes Otsuka's (2005) earlier argument:

> We must not enter the field with a set of theoretical assumptions in mind in the first place. We must avoid careless development of theoretical assumptions and the application of theories. Instead, we must be sensitive and honest to what the field tells us. (216)

In their opinion, area-studies-based epistemology and methodology are better suited to demonstrating 'humbleness and respect to the field', one of the key characteristics of quality comparative education in JCES (Morishita, Hattori, and Kamogawa 2013; Otsuka 2005; Yamada and Liu 2011).

This call for a 'respectful' attitude to the field is tied to their epistemological critique of social science theory. Leading JCES scholars have long criticised deductive, theoretically driven comparative education scholarship, and its uncritical use of social science theories and methodologies (see Maedaira and 1992; Otsuka 2005; Umakoshi 1992, 2007). JCES scholars conceive area-studies phenomenology and fieldwork as the key to 'liberate (themselves) from the spell of Eurocentric thoughts' (Ayabe 1975, 23; see also Otsuka 2005; Umakoshi 2007). They strongly condemn the uncritical adoption of Western theor-etical constructs, and argue that this perpetuates the legacy of Western Orientalism (Maedaira and 1992; Ninomiya and Maedaira 1990; Otsuka 2005; Umakoshi 1992, 2007; Yoshida 1990), or what Umakoshi (2001, 60) calls 'another form of ethnocentrism' – the perpetuation of Eurocentric knowledge as 'universal' by non-Western scholars like themselves (see also Otsuka 2005 for a similar view). Theory-driven comparative inquiries (the form of research more readily accepted in paradigmatic comparative education) prioritise theoretical integrity and coherent interpretation at the expense of understanding the lived experience of the 'locals', describing complexities on the ground, and interpreting reality in multiple ways (see Ninomiya 2001; Nishino 2011; Ogawa 2013).[6]

This acceptance of a description-heavy area-studies approach contrasts with a rather unfavourable assessment of the same by Anglo-American comparativists such as Cummings (1999), Epstein (1988), and Val Rust and his associates (1999). They problematise it for its lack of an explicit comparative methodology and theory. Though these shortcomings were also identified by Umakoshi (1992, 2007; see also Chikada 2011), the description-heavy area-studies approach remains privileged in JCES. It shapes the nature of postgraduate training, the criteria used to decide the annual outstanding dissertation for JCES's prestigious Hiratsuka Prize, and which articles get published in the society's flagship journal (Chikada 2011; Yamada 2011; Yamada and Liu 2011).[7]

Becoming 'dangerous' comparativists

The Japanese area-study comparativists interviewed for my study all draw upon this well-established intellectual tradition. All five area specialists are highly critical of the theory-driven research work that they consider characterises European and North American comparative education scholarship. Many doubt the empirical validity of such scholarship, as theory-driven inquiries lack descriptive detail. They see little value in reading research articles published in the English-language comparative education journals. Miwa, a specialist on a South-American country, argues:

> Many published articles in journals like *Comparative Education* and *Compare*, for instance, are very much theory-driven, and more often than not it feels they are simply fitting data into the pre-existing theoretical frameworks. They read well because arguments are very coherently presented, but they tend to distort the reality on the ground. So, I do not get much out of those studies.

This view is echoed by Hana, a South East Asian country specialist, who thinks that research articles published in the English-language journals are 'very shallow', as 'almost 60% of the articles are filled with the discussion of theory and research methodology'. As she reads these articles, she wonders 'where are the original research findings of the authors?'

To Tatsuo, another comparativist specialising in South Asian education, careful description of a given education phenomenon, or in his words, 'writing a dictionary' of it, is the primary purpose of comparative research. He contrasts this approach with what he considers to be the Western approach to comparative education, where focus is placed on analysis and theory building; 'instead of making a dictionary, they analyse the dictionary to identify patterns in its voluminous pages'. He maintains:

> Theory is not something you can carelessly play with when you are young. Theory development is something you might be able to engage in after years of fieldwork in a wide range of contexts. And theory is not something you try to develop alone.

Theory is thus considered something that grows from years of fieldwork, not the other way round, whereby theories are imposed from other disciplines upon the field. And it is something to be developed through collective effort. Hana also concurs with this, maintaining that theory is something that might emerge 'at the compilation of one's lifetime's work (*shutaisei*), perhaps after 20 years of fieldwork, not something that one should deal with in one's PhD dissertation'.

As Kamogawa (2010) and Yamada and Liu (2011) note, many area-study comparativists consider the process of research to be driven by the desire to understand its context, or rather, as a form of 'fact-finding'. Any prioritisation of a specific agenda and focus identified in advance by funding agents and through theoretical consideration is to be avoided. Rejecting the instrumentalist and purposeful approach to data collection as 'exploitative' (Sugimura, 2011, 272) , they propose 'wandering' or walking as a way to immerse oneself in the local context. The direct experience of 'smell, noise and the air' attainable only through an extended period of residence is deemed essential to understand the lived world and social space within which those being studied reside (Morishita, Hattori, and Kamogawa 2013, 220).

It is at this point that fieldwork assumes a profound ontological significance to these area-studies scholars. To Hana, fieldwork, when taken seriously, allows for a disintegration of researchers' pre-existing views, theories and their subjectivities. It is a deeply transformational process after which they come to 'appreciate the field as it presents itself'. Hana believes that English-language comparative researchers do not spend enough time in the field 'to allow for self-disintegration', the condition she believes is fundamental to self-objectification and thus a fully reflexive and contextualised approach to research (see also Otsuka 2005, 261 for a similar view). Here, anthropologist Tim Ingold's (2013, 4) insight is perceptive:

> It is almost a truism to say that there can be no description or documentation that is innocent of theory. But by the same token, no genuine transformation in ways of thinking and feeling is possible that is not grounded in close and attentive observation.

The JCES area-studies scholars' close attention to complexities and nuances on the ground is, hence, inseparably tied to the conceptualisation of fieldwork as a transformational process. As argued by Ingold (2013), this approach undercuts the empiricist premise of social science, the 'division between realms of knowing and of being' (5). The world and people that the JCES area-studies comparativists interact with through fieldwork exist, not just to be described and analysed, but to shape and reshape their being.

Interestingly, the same area-study comparativists are not ignorant of the discourse of paradigmatic comparative education, either. In fact, many used the English translation of key comparative education texts in their graduate seminars and were instructed to read the articles in English-language comparative education journals during their graduate studies. They confirm that it was common in Japanese graduate schools to organise seminars around a close reading of articles published in English-language journals such as *Comparative Education Review, Comparative Education* and *Compare*. As graduate students, they had to pick articles from the journals and present line by line translations. This practice has been inherited by some of the interviewees who now teach comparative and international education in the nation's leading institutions.

However, while engaging with English-language comparative education scholarship, these area-focused comparativists see little direct relevance of this practice to their actual scholarship. Hana recalls how her graduate seminars were organised around translation of English-language articles, including theoretical pieces by Rolland Paulston, Brian

Holmes, Philip Altbach, John Meyer and Jürgen Schriewer. She believes the whole purpose of the exercise was for graduate students to become familiar with the research trends in North America and Europe and to practise English-language translation. At the graduate seminars, she recalls, there was virtually no discussion of the content of the articles; the discussion focused on the accuracy of their translations.

Many area-focused researchers echo Hana's observations. During her graduate studies, Ayako saw considerable disjunction between Japanese and English-language comparative scholarship to the extent that, she says, 'it was not that meaningful' to read the latter. Pressed to identify one scholarly merit in this practice, Tatsuo, a specialist of a South Asian country, comments that it was good practice to 'acquire culture' (*kyoyo*), an expression that Ayako also uses. To these scholars, translation practice was not a total waste of time because it helped them improve their English-language skills, become familiar with the current research work outside Japan, and ensured that they 'will not be embarrassed when we go to international conferences'. All these participants confess, however, that the knowledge of the English-language comparative education gained through these translation practices did not influence their dissertation research in any significant way. As noted by Morishita, Hattori, and Kamogawa (2013), graduate students in Japanese institutions learned the theoretical work (Altbach, Carnoy and Paulston) in the late 1980s and the 1990s purely as 'Western debates' (214).

But these comparativists did not adopt the area-studies approach to comparative education research from the very beginning of their professional careers. When they started their graduate studies, many were more theoretically oriented and ambitious. For instance, both Hana and Masashi, a South East Asian country specialist, confessed that they were initially interested in social theorists popular at the time; Basil Bernstein, Pierre Bourdieu and Anthony Giddens, and wanted to apply their theoretical frameworks to the analysis of the education systems of South East Asian countries. Their dissertation supervisors, however, rejected their initial proposals. Hana was shocked and disappointed at her supervisor's reaction; 'you won't need such rubbish'. Instead, she was told to spend at least two consecutive years in the country of her choice and develop proficiency in the local language. Likewise, Masashi, pursuing his PhD degree in another leading comparative education research institute, felt that his initial proposal to be completely rejected by his supervisor, as he was told to put aside theories and go to live in the country for a year. However, after spending a few years in the respective countries of their choice in South East Asia, both Hana and Masashi had come to appreciate the importance of deep understanding of the context and to recognise the serious limitations of theoretically driven research that they had initially proposed. Masashi also describes the difficulty he faced attempting to have his work published in JCER as a critical turning point. Through the editorial committee's feedback on his rejected manuscripts, he gradually came to realise JCER's preference for a particular kind of comparative research and accordingly shifted the emphasis from theory to factual descriptions in his manuscript. In his final attempt, he completely removed any theoretical language from his work and was finally accepted for publication.

To Ayako, the process of 'unlearning theory' took place more gradually. Just like Masashi and Hana, she was theoretically inclined in her undergraduate studies. She enrolled in a graduate programme in comparative education in one of the leading national universities, and wanted to expand the theoretical framework of the relationship between modernisation and education systems informed by Talcott Parsons and Peter Berger. However, she soon realised that her initial research ideas were not the kind to be well received by her senior peers. Her supervisor also showed little understanding of or appreciation for her theoretically informed work. Eventually, she came to realise the limits of her theoretically driven research and the cognitive violence associated with it, and so fully adopted the Japanese area-study tradition.[8]

But not everyone trained in the area-studies tradition agrees with this atheoretical approach. Taro, a researcher specialising in a South Asian country, undertook strongly theoretical research work in both his Masters and PhD, informed by a theory dominant in the North American comparative education at the time. He admits that he was 'extremely exceptional' among the JCES comparativists of his generation. Unlike others, he did not choose the country of his specialisation early in his graduate training and instead spent time engaging with theoretical work in paradigmatic comparative education. Unlike the area-focused comparativists, he was not discouraged by his supervisor; he was encouraged to critically engage with theorists in Europe and North America. To him, graduate seminars where various theorists were read and translated in English were extremely meaningful and directly relevant to his PhD dissertation. He remains highly critical of the description-heavy empirical work in JCES that, in his opinion, has disconnected itself from the international community of comparative education. He argues that more interpretative and theoretically informed research should be pursued by Japanese comparative researchers, though he clearly recognises his view to be unpopular in JCES.

Such an attempt to be part of the 'international' conversation is hardly embraced by the area-focused comparative scholars. They have little desire to have their scholarship published in English in international scholarly journals. Instead, they are more interested in returning favours to the countries and communities in which they undertake fieldwork (Kamogawa 2010). This is part of their long-term commitment to the people in the country and the specific community in that country that they study. Indeed, none of the leading Japanese area-study comparativists are recognised in English-language paradigmatic comparative education, and yet they are recognised in the countries of their specialisation, and often invited as foreign experts on their education systems. Indeed, the view that 'you have not made it as a researcher, until your work is recognised by researchers in the country you study' (Ogawa 2013, 393) is widely shared among the area specialists. This suggests the existence of scholarly interactions and exchanges that entirely bypass paradigmatic comparative education.

Towards cross-culturalising comparative education

This discussion has shown how differently comparative education is conceptualised and practised within a particular intellectual tradition of JCES, in comparison to paradigmatic comparative education. But it is wrong to assume that what is described here is something specific to Japan; many Asian comparative education scholars are trained in Japanese institutions, and JCES plays a prominent role in the Comparative Education Society of Asia (Morishita, Kuroda, and Kitamura 2013, 42–43; also Mochida 2007).

Fact-finding, or 'dictionary-making' comparative scholarship, is widely practised in many parts of Asia and beyond. As highlighted in this paper, its lack of theoretical engagement does not result from its unfamiliarity with, or inability to understand, theory but from its epistemological critique of theory. Unfortunately, this critical insight is often unrecognised when their description-heavy phenomenological studies are assessed for publication in so-called international journals. They are often misrecognised as 'underdeveloped' or even 'unintelligible' by paradigmatic comparative scholarship, where theoretical and methodological insights and contributions are viewed as one of the most important, if not the only, criterion for quality scholarship (see Takayama 2011). Furthermore, my discussion has shown how the Eurocentric lineage of comparative education and JCES's marginality have created a particular intellectual context out of which the area-focused approach to comparative education gained traction as a viable alternative. The adoption of the area-studies approach was part of the strategy to reject paradigmatic comparative education's favoured mode of knowledge and so challenge the Western metropole's universality.

This discussion has also shown the possibility of using the critical insights generated in the margin to provincialise research as conceptualised in paradigmatic comparative education. Though we should refrain from over-generalising here, it is safe to suggest that the reliance on social science theoretical tools is widely accepted in paradigmatic comparative education; it continues to draw heavily on the theoretical tool kits of sociology, anthropology, political science and economics, and as suggested by Umakoshi (1992, 2007) places itself in a perpetual state of intellectual dependency on other more established disciplines. Here, a much more cautious treatment of social science theoretical constructs among JCES scholars is insightful. Their reservations about the universalist premises of social science theoretical knowledge have grown out of JCES scholars' struggle to assert their own intellectual and epistemological autonomy. In the words of Kuan-Hsing Chen (2010), the area-focused researchers reject the 'worship of theory' (226) where universalism is assumed to be 'an epistemological given' (245). Instead, they view universalism as 'a horizon we may be able to move towards in the remote future, provided that we first compare notes based upon locally grounded knowledge' (245). This epistemological modesty, or diffidence, expressed in Chen's work, underpins their 'dictionary-making' approach to comparative education research and their particular conceptualisation of fieldwork.

But the JCES area-study scholars' caution and often outright rejection of theoretical work also has its limitations. Indeed, despite Umakoshi's (1992, 2007) much-quoted call for interaction between fieldwork and theory, many area-focused JCES scholars, if not all, focus almost exclusively on providing detailed description of the phenomenon under study (Chikada 2011), or what Umakoshi (2007) calls 'excessive attachments to the area and unreflective cultural relativism' (60). This has resulted in a bifurcated intellectual context where theoretical tools, drawn from paradigmatic comparative education, are studied and yet hardly integrated into empirical work. Theoretical and methodological trends in the centre are treated as objects of study in and of themselves, as opposed to being utilised as a set of tools in research. This has left little room for the kind of critical engagement with theory for further refinement, modification and reconstruction proposed by Umakoshi (1992, 2007).[9] Another limitation of the JCES approach is the use of binary comparisons in their articulation of the 'uniquely Japanese' comparative research methodology (e.g. Ogawa 2013). The articulation of something 'uniquely Japanese' resorts to binary contrasting between what is 'uniquely Japanese' and what is putatively 'Western', but this is the identical trope mobilised by Japanese cultural nationalists. Hence, JCES scholars remain trapped with the postcolonial infatuation with the West and the nativist politics of resentment where theory is resisted on nationalistic grounds (Chen 2010, 226; see also Umakoshi 2007, 60).

Chakrabarty (2000, 19) writes that 'the categories and strategies we have learned from European thought … are both indispensable and inadequate' in presenting the particular historical experience of a non-Western modernity. They are simultaneously indispensable and inadequate, and the task of comparative scholars at the intellectual periphery is to critically engage with them (Yang 2011), so that their inadequacies are illuminated and concepts and frameworks are radically reconstituted, in this case, through the extensive fieldwork undertaken by JCES scholars. In response to the similar nativist response in Chinese education scholarship, Rui Yang (2011) argues that 'without engaging proactively with the dominant knowledge, the development of non-Western alternatives is almost empty talk' (402). Perhaps his insight is relevant to some corners of area-focused JCES scholars whose articulation of 'uniquely Japanese' comparative tradition echoes with the nativist politics of resentment.

Lastly, this discussion highlights the need to look to other, peripheral comparative educations and their 'subversive' intellectual traditions as a source of radical possibilities, epistemic – as opposed to empirical – others with whom the unnamed and unlocated nature of knowledge generated out of paradigmatic comparative education is exposed. A similar investigation into 'dangerous' traditions in other national, regional, language-based comparative education societies should be undertaken to open up the field for different methodological norms and conventions. Such an effort must be pursued with an attempt to alter the very institutional reality of uneven power relations in the field so that the field of comparative education will be thoroughly cross-culturalised; where the methodological, ontological and epistemological diversities of the world of comparative educations can be fully recognised and deployed for future generations of new research imaginations.

Notes

1. Similarly, there exist divergent intellectual trends within paradigmatic comparative education (see Cowen 1996, 2000; Epstein 1988; Rust et al. 1999; Manzon 2011). This surely problematises the rather monolithic representation of paradigmatic comparative education in my discussion. The issue raised here relates to the paradoxical tension between international relativism and intra-national relativism, which I have explored elsewhere (see Takayama 2016).
2. It is also notable that this methodological shift coincided with the emergence of public perception in Japan that catching up with the West was over, as Japan had achieved economic prosperity surpassing Western nations. With its economic might, Japanese government began its active involvement in international aid works in 'underdeveloped' countries via the Japanese International Cooperation Agency. The JCES's shift towards Asia and other less economically developed nations must be understood in this shift in Japan's geopolitical role and the availability of funding to comparative researchers specialising in this part of the world.
3. The view of social science theory as elitist or metropolitan-centric is shared among many Japanese area-study scholars specialising in South East Asia. See for instance Tsurumi's (1995) influential scholarship on 'periphery studies' (henkyogaku). It is well known that the same critical insight drove the Subaltern Studies in India (see Chakrabarty 2000).
4. Umakoshi (1992, 25) deems 'rather naïve' Altbach's view of comparative education as a field where theories developed in other social sciences (e.g. sociology) are applied in understanding different national and regional contexts of education. In a manner that clearly distinguishes himself from Altbach, Umakoshi calls for recognising comparative education as a

discipline that has its own methods, and he sees the integration of area-studies methods as a way to establish comparative education as a 'proper' discipline.

5. It is relevant to point out that Umakoshi translated many of the English-language comparative education scholarship that focuses on theoretical and methodological issues, including the works by Schriewer (2000) (see Umakoshi 2007, 43).

6. The atheoretical and strongly empirically based nature of Japanese social science scholarship in comparison to more theory-driven American and European counterparts is also recognised in the field of anthropology. In this sense, the stress on descriptive accuracy, precision and comprehensiveness can be interpreted as something particular not simply to JCES but to Japanese and, possibly, Asian social science in general (see Mathews 2008).

7. The majority of the Hiratsuka Awards winners are area-studies comparative researchers specialising in South East Asian countries. This suggests that JCES has long encouraged field-based comparative research in the region (Morishita, Kuroda, and Kitamura 2013, 37).

8. Likewise, overseas-trained comparative scholars experienced similar unlearning experiences upon their return to Japan. Takeshi, a UK-trained JCES researcher, remembers that the JCER review committee explained to him that the comparative analysis of three European countries in his submitted manuscript had finally been accepted for publication because of the new information about one of the countries that he added upon the review panel's request. He felt that the panel completely missed what he thought was the strength of the study, that is, the new analytical insights generated through the three-nation comparison.

9. According to Shigetaka Imai (1999), who introduced the theoretical debate (Meyer's world culture theory, Wallerstein's world systems theory and Luhmann's system theory) to Japanese readers and also translated (with Umakoshi) *Discourse formation in comparative education* edited by Schriewer (2000), his writing and translation generated absolutely no response among the JCES scholars (Personal communication, May 2013).

Disclosure statement

No potential conflict of interest was reported by the author.

References

Appadurai, A. 2000. "Grassroots Globalization and the Research Imagination." *Public Culture* 12 (1): 1–19. doi:10.1215/08992363-12-1-1.

Ayabe, T. 1975. "Nihon no hikakukyouikugaku no kenkyuuhouhouronjou no shomondai [Various Issues with Research Methodology in Japanese Comparative Education]." *Hikakukyouikugaku kenkyuu* [Comparative Education] 1: 23–29.

Bray, M. 2002. "Comparative Education in East Asia." *Current Issues in Comparative Education* 4 (2): 70–80.

Bray, M. 2003a. "Tradition, Change, and the Role of the World Council of Comparative Education Societies." *International Review of Education* 49 (1–2): 1–13. doi:10.1023/A:1022946730474.

Bray, M. 2003b. "Comparative Education in the Era of Globalization." *Policy Futures in Education* 1 (2): 209–224. doi:10.2304/pfie.2003.1.2.2.

Bray, M., and M. Manzon. 2014. "The Institutionalization of Comparative Education in Asia and the Pacific: Roles and Contributions of Comparative Education Societies and the WCCES." *Asia Pacific Journal of Education* 34 (2): 228–248. doi:10.1080/02188791.2013.875646.

Chakrabarty, D. 2000. *Provincializing Europe: Postcolonial Thought and Historical Difference.* Princeton, NJ: Princeton University Press.

Chen, K. 2010. *Asia as Method: Toward De-imperialization.* Durham, NC: Duke University Press.

Chikada, M. 2011. "Hikakukyoikugakuno Jirenmato Kanosei [Dilemma and Possibility of Comparative Education]." *Hikakukyoikugakukenkyu* [Comparative Education] 42: 111–123.

Chikada, M. 2011. "hikaku kyouikugaku no jirenma to kanousei [Dilemma and Possibility of Comparative Education]." *Hikakukyouikugaku kenkyuu* [Comparative Education] 42: 111–123.

Connell, R. 2007. *Southern Theory: The Global Dynamics of Knowledge in Social Science.* Crows Nest, NSW: Allen & Unwin.

Cowen, R. 1996. "Last Past the Post: Comparative Education, Modernity and Perhaps Postmodernity." *Comparative Education* 32 (2): 151–170. doi:10.1080/03050069628812.

Cowen, R. 2000. "Comparing Futures or Comparing Pasts?" *Comparative Education* 36 (3): 333–342.

Cummings, W. 1999. "The Institutions of Education: Compare, Compare, Compare!" *Comparative Education Review* 43: 413–437. doi:10.1086/447578.

Ehara, T. 2001. "Tokushu: Chiikikyoikukenkyunofuronta, tokushunoshushi [Special Issue: The Frontier of Area Studies of Education. Introduction]." *Hikakukyoikugakukenkyu* [Comparative Education] 27: 4.

Epstein, E. H. 1988. "The Problematic Meaning of 'Comparison' in Comparative Education." In *Theories and Methods in Comparative Education*, edited by J. Schriewer and B. Holmes, 3–23. Frankfurt am Main: Peter Lang.

Hokari, M. 2011. *Gurindji Journey: A Japanese Historian in the Outback.* Sydney: University of New South Wales Press.

Imai, S. 1999. "Hikakukyoikugakunonyufurontia [New Frontiers in Comparative Education]." *Hikakukyoikugakukenkyu* [Comparative Education] 25: 5–15.

Ingold, T. 2013. *Making: Anthropology, Archaeology, Art and Architecture.* London: Routledge.

Ishii, S., and T. Umakoshi. 1990. "Nihon ni okeru hikakukyouikugaku kenkyuu [Comparative Education in Japan]." In *Hikakukyouikugaku* [Comparative Education], edited by M. Yoshida, 48–62. Tokyo: Fukumura shuppan.

Ishizuki, M. ed. 2001. *Hikaku kokusai kyouikugaku* [Comparative and International Education]. Tokyo: Toushindou.

Kamogawa, A. 2010. "Furoku: Morujibufirudotenmatsuki [Appendix: Note on Maldives Fieldwork]." http://www.gsid.nagoya-u.ac.jp/syamada/linkpages/researchproject/kakenreport07.pdf

Kitamura, Y. 2005. "Hikakukyoikugakutokaihatsukenkyunokakawari [The Engagement Between Comparative Education and Development Studies]." *Hikakukyoikugakukenkyu* [Comparative Education] 31: 241–252.

Kobayashi, T. 1975. "Nihonnohikakukyoikugakunokenkyuhohojonoshomondai [Issues of Japanese Comparative Education Research Methodology]." *Hikakukyoikugakukenkyu* [Comparative Education] 1: 10–12.

Maedaira, Y. 1992. "Le Tan Koi: Esunosentorizumuokoerumono. [Le Tan Koi: Beyond Ethnocentricism.]." In *Hikakukyoikugaku* [Comparative Education], edited by L. T. Koi and translated by Y. Maedaira, 417–436. Kyoto: Korosha.

Manzon, M. 2011. *Comparative Education: The Construction of a Field.* Hong Kong: Comparative Education Research Centre, The University of Hong Kong.

Manzon, M., and M. Bray. 2006. "The Comparative and International Education Society (CIES) and the World Council of Comparative Education Societies (WCCES)." *Current Issues in Comparative Education* 8 (2): 69–83.

Masemann, V., M. Bray, and M. Manzon, eds. 2007. *Common Interests, Uncommon Goals: Histories of the World Council of Comparative Education Societies and Its Members.* Hong Kong: Comparative Education Research Centre, The University of Hong Kong. Dordrecht: Springer.

Mathews, G. 2008. "Why Japanese Anthropology Is Ignored Beyond Japan." *Japanese Review of Cultural Anthropology* 9: 53–69.

Mochida, K. 2007. "The Comparative Education Society of Asia (CESA)." In *Common Interests, Uncommon Goals: Histories of the World Council of Comparative Education Societies and its Members*, edited by V. Masemann, M. Bray, and M. Manzon, 309–315. Hong Kong: Comparative Education Research Centre, The University of Hong Kong.

Morishita, M., M. Hattori, and A. Kamogawa. 2013. "Teiseitekishuhoomochiitahikakukyoikugakukenkyu [Comparative Education Research: Ethnographic Approach]." In *Hikakukyoikugakunochihei ohiraku* [Opening up New Horizons in Comparative Education], edited by S. Yamada and M. Morishita, 209–223. Tokyo: Toshindo.

Morishita, M., K. Kuroda, and Y. Kitamura. 2013. "Sekainonakanonihonhikakukyoikugaku – Gakumonrontokenkyujittai [JCES in the World: Disciplinary Debates and the State of Research]." In *Hikakukyoikugakunochiheiohiraku* [Opening Up New Horizons in Comparative Education], edited by S. Yamada and M. Morishita, 20–46. Tokyo: Toshindo.

Niibori, M. 1975. "Nihonnohikakukyoikunokenkyuhohohoronjonoshomondai–Kyoiku shakaigakuteki apurochi [Issues with Research Methodology in Japanese Comparative Education – Insights from the Sociology of Education Approach]." *Hikakukyoikugakukenkyu* [Comparative Education] 1: 17–22.

Ninomiya, A. 2001. "Hikakukokusaikyoikunoayumi [The Trajectory of Comparative and International Education]." In *hikakukokusaikyoikugaku* [Comparative and International Education], edited by M. Ishizuki, 22–41. Tokyo: Toshindo.

Ninomiya, A., and Y. Maedaira. 1990. "Hikakukyoikugakunokenkyuho [Research Methods of Comparative Education]." In *Hikakukyoikugaku* [Comparative Education], edited by M. Yoshida, 27–47. Tokyo: Fukumura shuppan.

Nishino, S. 2011. "Kokusaikyoikukaihatsutohikakukyoikugakukenkyunokanosei [Possibilities of International Educational Development and Comparative Studies of Education]." *Hikakukyoikugakukenkyu* [Comparative Education] 42: 124–139.

Ogawa, Y. 2013. "Higashiajiaomiruhikakukyoikugaku [Comparative Studies of East Asian Education]." In *Hikakukyoikugakunochiheiohiraku* [Opening up New Horizons in Comparative Education], edited by S. Yamada and M. Morishita, 380–397. Tokyo: Toshindo.

Okihara, Y., ed. 1981. *Hikakukyoikugaku* [Comparative Education]. Tokyo: Yushindo kobunsha.

Otsuka, Y. 1994. "Kyoikunochiikikenkyu (Omonihiseiyo) [Area Studies of Education (Non-Western World)]." *Hikakukyoikugakukenkyu* [Comparative Education] 20: 41–47.

Otsuka, Y. 2005. "Hohotoshitenofiirudo [Field as a Research Method]." *Hikakukyoikugakukenkyu* [Comparative Education] 31: 253–263.

Otsuka, Y. 2005. "Houhoutoshiteno fiirudo [Field as a Research Method]." *Hikakukyouikugaku kenkyuu* [Comparative Education] 31: 253–263.

Rappleye, J., and H. Komatsu. 2015. "Living on Borrowed Time: Rethinking Temporality, Self, Nihilism, and Schooling." *Comparative Education* 52 (2): 177–201. doi:10.1080/03050068.2016.1142736.

Rust, V. D., A. Soumaré, O. Pescador, and M. Shibuya. 1999. "Research Strategies in Comparative Education." *Comparative Education Review* 43 (1): 86–109. doi:10.1086/447546.

Schriewer, J. 2000. *Discourse Formation in Comparative Education*. Frankfurt am Main: Peter Lang.

Sugimura, M. 2011. "Nihonniokeruhikakukyoikukenkyunohohoronomegurugiron[Debates over Comparative Education Methodology in Japan]." In *Comparative Education Research: Approaches and Methods* (Translated by M. Sugimura, Y. Yamato, M. Maeda, and T. Ako), edited by B. Mark, B. Adamson, and M. Mason, 259–292. Tokyo: Sophia University Press.

Takayama, K. 2011. "A Comparativist's Predicaments of Writing About 'Other' Education: A Self-reflective, Critical Review of Studies of Japanese Education." *Comparative Education* 47 (4): 449–470. doi:10.1080/03050068.2011.561542.

Takayama, K. 2015. "Provincializing and Globalizing the World Culture Theory Debate: Critical Insights from a Margin." *Globalisation, Societies and Education* 13 (1): 34–57. doi:10.1080/14767724.2014.967485.

Takayama, K. 2016. "Deploying the Post-colonial Predicaments of Researching on/with 'Asia' in Education: A Standpoint from a Rich Peripheral Country." *Discourse: Studies in the Cultural Politics of Education* 37 (1): 70–88. doi:10.1080/01596306.2014.927114.

Takayama, K., A. Sriprakash, and R. Connell. 2017. "Rethinking Knowledge Production and Circulation in Comparative and International Education: Southern Theory, Postcolonial Perspectives, and Alternative Epistemologies." *Comparative Education Review* 61 (S1): 1–24. doi:10.1086/690455.

Tsurumi, Y. 1995. *Tonanajiaoshiru – Watashinohoho* [Understanding South East Asia – My Method]. Tokyo: Iwanami Shoten.

Umakoshi, T. 1992. "Area Studies as the Foundation of Comparative Education." *Bulletin of the School of Education, Nagoya University (Dept. of Education)* 39 (2): 21–29.

Umakoshi, T. 2001. "Hikakukokusaikyoikugakukenkyunogenzai [The Present State of Comparative and International Education]." In *Hikakukokusaikyoikugaku* [Comparative and International Education], edited by M. Ishizuki, 42–59. Tokyo: Toshindo.

Umakoshi, T. 2007. *Hikakukyoikugaku: Ekkyonoressun* [Comparative Education: Lessons for Border-Crossing]. Tokyo: Toushindou.

Yamada, S. 2011. "Nihonnohikakukyoikugakuniokerudentototayouka [The Tradition and Diversity in Japanese Comparative Education]." *Hikakukyoikugakukenkyu* [Comparative Education] 42: 140–158.

Yamada, S., and J. Liu. 2011. "Between Epistemology and Research Practices: Emerging Research Paradigms and the Tradition of Japanese Comparative Education." In *Beyond the Comparative*, edited by J. Weidman and J. J. William, 371–394. New York: Sense.

Yang, R. 2011. "Educational Research in Confucian Cultural Contexts: Reflections on Methodology." *Comparative Education* 47 (3): 395–405.

Yoshida, M. 1990. "Hikakukyouikugaku towa nanika [What Is Comparative Education?]." In *Hikakukyouikugaku* [Comparative Education], edited by M. Yoshida, 11–26. Tokyo: Fukumura shuppan.

Comparative education histories: a postscript

Maria Manzon ⓘD

ABSTRACT
Comparative education is two centuries old. Many mainstream historical narratives claim that the field began with the iconic opus of Marc-Antoine Jullien de Paris (1817). This article offers to re-theorise the histories of comparative education. It suggests casting a far-sighted and panoramic look at the field's origins. An underlying assumption in these histories is the embeddedness of comparative education in ever-changing world orders. The article concludes with a puzzle for future work on a global history of comparative education.

Introduction

Historical narratives of academic disciplines and fields vary in interpretation depending on the lenses used. Orthodox disciplinary histories typically adopt tropes of unity and cumulative progress as in a linear, unidirectional and teleological fashion, while critical postmodernist and poststructuralist stances portray disruptive and discontinuous histories. Klein (1993, 196) claimed that disciplinary histories play several representative functions, such as socialising novices into a field, legitimating the field to outsiders, and managing change. Disciplinary histories seek to legitimate political interests in battles for intellectual territory with neighbouring academic tribes (Becher and Trowler 2001). This can be achieved by extending 'the present (or what is to become the future) as far as possible into the past, thereby constructing an image of continuity, consistency and determinacy' (Graham, Lepenies, and Weingart 1983, xvii).

Critical theorists view these patterns with suspicion. They query narratives that claim to establish the 'official' historical stages of development of any discipline or disseminate 'founder narratives' as discursive moves to legitimate political territories (Klein 1993). This article celebrates the bicentenary of what is widely regarded as comparative education's foundational text (Jullien 1817) yet problematises the field's beginnings.

Plato's *Allegory of the cave* (1963) is a useful starting point for this critical review. It describes some prisoners who are bound deep in a cave and who have not seen the light of day. Their limited vision can only capture shadows which they misconstrue as reality. They are unaware that things of greater reality lie beyond their cave. Histories of comparative education somewhat resemble this limited view. They are sometimes constrained and partial representations of a greater, complex and dynamic reality. This article aims to contrast those shadows in the histories of comparative education with the greater reality that they imperfectly reflect.

This article has three main sections. The first section reviews the types of histories in the archives. The second offers a critique of some 'orthodox' histories in order to open further pathways for a more global historical narrative of the field. The article closes with some thoughts on how some as yet unwritten histories might look like within an evolving world order.

Written histories

The existing literature on the histories of comparative education can be classified into four types:

(1) *Intellectual history* as a series of epistemological, methodological and theoretical stages;
(2) *Institutional history* as a tracing of the development of university programs, specialist publications, professional societies, and other comparative education institutions;
(3) *Genealogy* as a history of a school of thought over several generations, tracing the lineage from masters to their disciples; and
(4) *Discursive history* as a history of the kinds of statements that authors deploy when purporting to write the history of a field or to comment on its nature and future.

There are overlaps in this typology. Some histories in the field of comparative education combine one or several types (e.g. Altbach 1991; Cowen and Kazamias 2009; Crossley and Watson 2003; García Garrido 1996; Gottlieb 2000; Halls 1990; Manzon 2011). Of these, the globally comprehensive volume edited by Halls (1990) is an outstanding early work. Some of these are critical narratives: they examine power-knowledge relations in the development of the field. Oral histories have also been documented in audio-visual medium (e.g. CIES 2006, 2016). Theoretical approaches vary from historiography, philosophy of history, sociology, among others.

Intellectual histories

Historical narratives of this genre include those that trace the epistemological roots and currents of the field (e.g. Epstein 2008; Kazamias 2009), the grand theories and disciplinary approaches that hegemonised particular time periods (e.g. Ferrer 2002; Paulston 1994; Wang 1999; Weidman and Jacob 2011; Welch 1997), the main themes and methodological approaches employed in specific periods (e.g. Bereday 1964; Kelly, Altbach, and Arnove 1982), and the salient forms and/or purposes of comparative education (e.g. García Garrido 1996; Gu 2001; Noah and Eckstein 1969; Phillips and Schweisfurth 2014). These histories commonly take the post-Enlightenment period as the field's starting point. It is closely associated with European traditions of travel and colonialism (Sobe 2017).

Less visible within the literature, concretely in the Anglophone discourses, are pioneers of the field in some parts of the world. For example, among the Latin American forerunners of comparative education in the nineteenth century were Andrés Bello (Venezuela), Domingo Faustino Sarmiento (Argentina), and José Pedro Varela (Uruguay) (Acosta and Ruiz 2017; Martínez 2013). Prominent Spanish authors include Ramón de la Sagra, Pablo Montesino, and Pedro Felipe Monlau (García Garrido 1996). In Japan, Fujimaro Tanaka (1843–1890) is considered a pioneer of the field (Takekuma 2008), and educational borrowing by the Arab World from the West was fostered in the early 1800s by Egyptian Mohamed Ali (Erlich 1989).

There is also a growing literature on iconographies of comparative education. Examples include research on the life and works of figures such as Matthew Arnold, Henry Barnard, Victor Cousin, Friedrich August Hechtius, Marc-Antoine Jullien, Horace Mann, and Michael Sadler (Epstein 2017; Kaloyannaki and Kazamias 2009; Lenhart 2016; 2017; Rapple 2017). Short biographies of twentieth-century comparativists have been written including C. Arnold Anderson, George Bereday, William Brickman, Isaac Kandel, Gerald Read (e.g. Adick 2017; Cowen 2017; Epstein 2016a; Robertson and Cushner 2016; Silova and Brehm 2014) and Chinese scholars (Hayhoe 2006). Another source of biographies is the collection of vignettes on historical and contemporary figures published in CIEclopedia,[1] an online who's who in comparative and international education. Occasionally, obituaries are published in specialist comparative education journals. For example, on Nicholas Hans (Holmes 1970), W.D. Halls (Phillips 2011), Edmund King (Broadfoot 2002), and Nigel Grant (Winther-Jensen 2004), and Julio Ruiz Berrio and Ferrán Ferrer (Lázaro 2014). Of particular interest is Cowen's proposal for a re-interpretation of the history of comparative education 'by reviewing the relationships between individual biography, professional work places (universities of the period) and personal "readings of the global" in the work of individual scholars as they responded to political and social worlds outside of the university' (2017, Conclusion, para. 1).

Institutional histories

Histories of the institutionalisation of comparative education as formal academic programs or coursework at universities and teacher training colleges, publication of specialist books and journals and formation of professional societies, typically comprise the literature on institutional histories. The earliest lecture course reported in the Anglophone literature is by James Russell at the Columbia University, USA in 1900 (Bereday 1963). Attempts to document institutional histories have been patchy, partial, ad hoc and sometimes implicitly biased towards favouring the position of the historiographer. But the literature is burgeoning. I list only a few here.

(a) histories of teaching at universities (e.g. Bergh and Soudien 2006; Bray and Gui 2001; García Garrido 1996; Halls 1990; Leclerq 1999; Marquina and Lavia 2007; Schwille 2017; Wolhuter et al. 2013).
(b) histories of professional societies and research centres (e.g. Epstein 2016b; Manzon 2015; Masemann, Bray, and Manzon 2007).
(c) histories of society journals (e.g. Bray 2010; Martínez and Valle 2005; Nordtveit 2016).
(d) festschrifts to honour senior scholars in the field (e.g. Albarea 2013; Kodron et al. 1997; Larsen 2010; Masemann et al. 2010; Weidman and Jacob 2011).

Genealogies

Writings of a family history genre, that is, not in the Foucauldian sense of the term, are probably much less common than institutional histories in the field of comparative education. Examples include Wilson (1994) and García Garrido (2005). Pertinent works on 'founding fathers' of comparative education include Rosselló (1943) and Vilanou and Valls (2001). Other personal histories of contemporary scholars include Cowen (2010), and Hayhoe (2006) which profiles two influential Chinese scholars in twentieth-century comparative education: Gu Mingyuan and Wang Chengxu. There are also short and long autobiographies (e.g. Adamson 2015; Gu 2005; Hayhoe 2004; Lee 2015; Yang 2015).

Discursive histories

Tracing the discourses about the history and nature of comparative education is a fairly new approach. Ninnes (2008) exemplifies this genre. In these narratives, discourses are used to define and limit a field of study, and thus constitute and reconstitute the field. In examining discursive histories, Ninnes is not as interested in the substantive content of disciplinary histories (who founded what, when and where) as he is in the discursive moves in these narrations (how particular names are presented), and on the impact these linguistic techniques have on policing the boundaries of the field and in legitimising its existence by determining a point of origin in space and time, and locating its origins as far back in time as possible. He urges future writers of disciplinary histories to be more inclusive, less eulogistic, to avoid linear and seamless evolutionary narratives, and instead to be reflective and aware of the partial and particular reading they offer of the field as well as of the impact their discourse has on re-constituting the field.

   Within this genre of writing, awareness is raised of the discursive moves of some historiographers of comparative education who take as a high point the 'founding' of their own school of thought. Such is the case of the developmental stages proposed by Noah and Eckstein (1969) who categorised the development of comparative education into five stages, the ultimate stage being the dominance of empirical quantitative research in comparative education.

Re-thinking 'histories'

This section elaborates a critical stance on the 'official', 'orthodox', 'paradigmatic' histories of comparative education in order to re-theorise the field's historiography. The aim is to open new pathways towards more inclusive global histories of the field. Discourse, taken in a Foucauldian sense, refers to a limited set of things that can be said and not said. I will expose some aspects that have not been said, or that may have been but are not as audible, in paradigmatic Anglophone historiography of comparative education.

   I borrow Nóvoa's (2009, 818) idea of 'multiplying spaces and unfolding times' in order to advance comparative historical work. It is similar to the thinking behind Chen's 'Asia as method', which proposes to 'multiply frames of reference in our subjectivity and worldview, so that our anxiety over the West can be diluted, and productive critical work can move forward' (Chen 2010, 223).

Similar perspectives have illuminated excellent recent scholarship in the field that critique the colonial entanglements of knowledge production in comparative education (Takayama, Sriprakash, and Connell 2017; also Silova, Millei, and Piattoeva 2017; Sobe 2017; Takayama 2017). However, following the tradition of post-colonial theory, for these critical scholars, 'Europe works as a silent referent in historical knowledge' (Chakrabarty 2000, 28). Their writing takes European colonialism in the modern era as the starting point of re-thinking the field of knowledge.

I argue, however, that in order to truly multiply spaces and frames of reference as well as unfold times, other eras of colonialism as well as pre-colonial periods in spaces other than Europe need to be remembered. At the same time, other educational *spaces* and knowledge paradigms need to be compared.

One recent move to look further back in history has been initiated by Epstein (2017). He proposes three criteria for determining the true origin of comparative education (2017, 326):

(1) the early manifestation of comparative study,
(2) the degree to which systematic study is performed, and
(3) the capacity for generalisation.

Although Epstein (2017) identified several potential founders of comparative education whose works were published between 1763 and 1795, and had therefore preceded Jullien's *Esquisse* (1817), they were all Europeans. Nevertheless, his three criteria for determining the origin of the field are useful and applicable to the re-conceptualisation of the origins of the field. That is, in new time zones and invisible spaces.

Refuting doxa

I offer three main critiques of routine orthodox histories. They confront reductionist assumptions that underlie comparative education historiography. They encompass perspectives on the nature of education, on paradigmatic space and time, and equitable discourse.

Historicising education

First, the concept of 'education' in many comparative education histories is almost synonymous to modern national education systems and formal schooling in the nineteenth century. However, why should 'education' be limited to 'formal schooling'? Does not education start in the home? Did not churches, mosques, and synagogues provide education too? How about shadow education? (Bray 2017). Even if education were limited to formal education, why is it limited to the post-Enlightenment period? As discussed in an earlier article on the historical origins of comparative education in Asia, the field is not 'monogenetic'; rather it has multiple origins in different parts of the world (Manzon 2017, 3). Educational institutions had existed and served as the seedbed of classical thought in ancient civilisations in Greece, China, and India, to name a few. There are, for example, the two major theological centres in the ancient Near East, the School of Antioch (Syria) and the School of Alexandria (Egypt), located in the major cities of the ancient Roman Empire, and the first madrasah in Mecca. They too form part of the history of education. It is highly plausible that some early forms of comparison of education would have taken place among ancient and medieval colonies and civilisations. Future research could provide evidence of 'older' pioneer comparativists based on the three criteria of Epstein (2017).

The above examples merely serve to make the point that the concept of 'education' viewed in comparative perspective needs to be broadened. Looking at earlier forms of educational institutionalisation before the nineteenth-century mass schooling systems can make visible new (albeit old) spaces of comparative education.

Multiplying space–time

A second critique relates to space–time coordinates. Paradigmatic narratives about the origins of comparative education in the paradigmatic histories tend to be located in the late eighteenth European space–time. The 'fathers' of comparative education were Europeans, for example, Marc-Antoine Jullien, Friedrich August Hecht, Christian Gottlob Heyne, and Louis-René de Caradeuc la Chalotais (Epstein 2017). They were based in Europe and borrowed ideas mainly from countries within Europe. There were also [North] American pioneers such as Horace Mann, Calvin Stowe and Henry Barnard who looked to European education for inspiration (Kaloyannaki and Kazamias 2009). However, Eurocentric historiography has been critiqued by Chakrabarty (2000). I offer alternative frames of reference for comparative education's genealogies by discussing the practice of cultural borrowing as an early manifestation of the field.

Educational transfer had been taking place in many parts of the world even prior to the nineteenth century. The spectrum of educational transfer proposed by Phillips and Ochs (2004) is useful here. There were varying degrees of voluntary and involuntary cross-cultural/cross-boundary influences on educational/knowledge transfer, be they colonial impositions, intentional policy borrowing, or the general influence of ideas – what Lenhart (2017) termed as 'transnationality'. These exchanges or influences took place from ancient times among the world's oldest civilisations, to Western colonialism and post-independence eras. Some of these moments of cultural borrowing in major world regions were documented in Halls (1990). I highlight that different periods in the world's history have seen various attempts or forms of colonialism or imperialism way before the modernist era. Why then does the discourse on comparative education construct it as a post-Enlightenment phenomenon in Europe? Spaces and times need to be multiplied. The following discusses a few new (yet old) zones.

In ancient East Asia, educational borrowing and lending by China go as far back as the Han Dynasty (206 BC to 220 AD). The Tang Dynasty (618–906 AD) witnessed the zenith of cosmopolitan culture, commercial trade especially along the Silk Road, and political hegemony over what is now called Japan, North and South Korea, and Vietnam. Asian states and Western countries looked to China for policy inspiration. For example, Japan's first national education system resulted from intentional importation after a diplomatic mission to China in 607 (Kobayashi 1990). Presumably, such purposeful copying of educational policy and institutional forms would not have been the result of mere traveller's tales but of systematic study of the other. The bidirectional flow of knowledge between India and China during the first millennium is also noteworthy. According to Sen (2004), Chinese scholars visited India especially during the Tang Dynasty (seventh century).

Among them was Xuanjang, a Chinese Buddhist monk and scholar who spent 16 years in India and studied at Nalanda, an ancient Indian institution of higher education in the fifth century. Indian scholars also visited China not only for religious motives but also for scientific knowledge.

In the middle ages, two noteworthy globalising or colonial powers were Christianity and Islam. The spread of Islamic civilisation between China and Spain (seventh to nineteenth centuries) and the establishment of intellectual centres of world learning such as the House of Wisdom in Baghdad (Iran) are but two examples of fertile soil for the investigation of educational comparison practices. Christianity too was a major force of cosmopolitanism and universality, including the use of Latin as a transnational language to promote unity in the Church that was spreading throughout the world. Missionaries served as bi-directional cultural bridges. Not only would they be vehicles of salvation but also of scientific knowledge. Conversely, they would also assimilate indigenous forms of knowing into their catechetical practices. Here is comparative (religious) education in action. Christianity was also a major force in intellectual cultivation. The medieval universities of the eleventh and twelfth centuries established in Bologna (Italy), Sorbonne (France) and Oxford (England) were born from the monastic schools and cathedral schools that dated back to the sixth century. These 'colonisers' have also encountered and dialogued with other cultures. Why could they not have witnessed early forms of comparative education?

Dialoguing with the 'other'

A third critique of orthodox histories is inequity in its discourses arising from the hegemony of English as the language of discourse, and the 'male-centredness' of its historical narratives.

Anderson (2004) in his work on nations as 'imagined communities', argued that one of the main causes of nationalism – the fragmentation of great classical communities – is the decline of Latin. It represented the breaking up of sacred communities who conceived of themselves as cosmically central, united by an old and sacred language. A common, transnational language unites; vernaculars divide.

Within comparative education, there are also 'imagined communities' who are separated from and sometimes unable to communicate with each other. Three articles in this volume attest to this. First, Adick (2017) demonstrates the linguistic divide evidenced in the unilateral pattern of citations of the work Bereday vis-a-vis Hilker. While both figures referenced each other (they were polyglots and were familiar with each other's work), succeeding generations in their respective language groupings – the Anglophone vs. Germanophone – aligned with either Bereday or Hilker and failed to recognise their shared paternity of the 'four steps of comparison' model. (García Garrido [1996] is one example of the exception to this practise: he cited both Bereday and Hilker with reference to the four-step model). Secondly, Takayama (2017), writing on 'area studies' practised by Japanese scholars also points to the imbalanced visibility of Japanese research traditions in Anglophone literature, but not the reverse. He describes this situation as 'asymmetric ignorance', borrowing the concept from Chakrabarty (2000, 28). In the case of the Japanese, however, Takayama (2017) also pointed to the gatekeeping practices in Anglophone journals which marginalised other research traditions (e.g. bias against not theory-based work). In third place, Acosta and Ruiz (2017) narrate international trends in the historical development of comparative education yet their sources are mainly in Spanish although similar contents were available in English. These are just a few examples of linguistic divides which constrain the work of comparative historiography. They also suggest the hegemony of English as the language of (published) scholarship (see e.g. critics from Macedo, Gounari, and Dendrinos 2003; Tietze and Dick 2013). The present article can be criticised for the relative absence of literature from less visible linguistic communities due to the author's language limitation as well. At the least, effort has been made to reach out to other discursive communities and represent them in the literature reviewed here, albeit not comprehensively. Certainly language is not the only the factor, and the pattern of citations is not only determined by language; political, intellectual affiliation may also intervene. Yet Anderson makes a clear point: 'print-capitalism created languages of power' (2004, 45).

Another form of 'imagined communities' in comparative education is its professional societies. Over 40 comparative education societies comprise the membership of the World Council of Comparative Education Societies (WCCES). They include national, regional, and language-based scholarly entities. The WCCES faces linguistic challenges, as other global bodies. Its use of English as the working language has marginalised some groups (Bray and Manzon 2014). As García Garrido (2004), a long-serving and active Spanish representative in the WCCES in the 1980s recalled, the SEEC (*Sociedad Española de Educación Comparada*) had not been visible in the WCCES forums in the 1990s, partly due to the linguistic barrier.

Apart from language biases, orthodox histories suffer from gender inequity. The iconic progenitors of the field are all males. Cowen (2009, 9) highlighted the need to make women visible in comparative historiography, such as Ann Dryland and Madame Hattinguais, to name two.

In the above, I have attempted to contest the orthodox histories of comparative education. I have sought to break away from the genealogies couched in Eurocentric, post-Enlightenment discourses. I examined three elements in the formula of comparative education history: 'education' * (space + time) * (equity of [language + gender]). A more complete history needs to re-conceptualise these elements.

Future puzzles

More broadly, the common thread that runs through the histories of comparative education is the relationship between power and knowledge (Manzon 2011; also Dale 2015). Comparative education histories have always been embedded in particular world orders. The 'place' and shape of comparative education metamorphoses according to the contours of the country's position in the world order. Substantial academic institutionalisation happened after the Second World War in countries that enjoyed a central locus of power in global economics and politics. Their education systems served as models for countries in other parts of the world. Education policy transfers fuelled the demand for trained comparativists. Inversely, comparative education was delegitimised in countries under totalitarian regimes which viewed comparative education knowledge as a threat due to their origins in countries that were their political foes. Alternatively, comparative education work was colonised by education planners and statisticians in, for example,

Latin America for purposes of educational expansion (Acosta and Ruiz 2017). Comparative education is thus particularly sensitive to the interplay between national and international politics (Cowen 2014) and economics.

World orders have influenced comparative education in the past. What then is the new world order in the 2020s and beyond? What would it mean for comparative education? China, for example, has become a major voice in international political and economic circles. Its 'One Belt, One Road' initiative aims to establish a China-centred global trading network as an alternative to 'Western-dominated' economies. Singapore and other developed Asian societies continue to attract study delegations not only from its Asian neighbours but also from Europe and North America. The points of reference for educational borrowing are shifting eastwards, that is, to the new East. There are now multiple points of reference and multiple bidirectional arrows. Similarly, knowledge production is 'becoming more multi-polar' and non-Western scholarship is growing in significance (Yang 2015, 61). One example is in the histories of comparative education societies, where the genealogical patterns are also shifting 'eastwards'. Initially, older and bigger comparative education societies (e.g. the Comparative and International Education Society, the Comparative Education Society in Europe, and the WCCES) served as catalysts of society formation in other regions (Manzon and Bray 2007). Yet, the Comparative Education Society in Asia is becoming a catalyst too of new national societies of comparative education within its own ambit (Bray and Manzon 2014). In view of these shifting positions of power, what would the new histories of the field look like 20, 30, 50 years down the road? Who will write them and where would their institutions be based? How would the great masters of twentieth-century comparative education 'read' these re-written histories of their times?

Second, what new 'zones of looking' (Nóvoa 2009, 819) and thus new understandings of comparative education can be explored? Why are pre-Enlightenment forms of comparative education knowledge excluded? If the present is the transformation of the past into the future, then the present is a compression of layers of the past. If so, then the so-called nineteenth-century progenitors of comparative education are not stand-alone, isolated heroes. They represent the compression of layers of other forerunners, cultures and epistemes of comparative educations in different spaces and times. Thicker and wider conceptions of time as well as plurality of space can emancipate current historical narratives.

Third, discursive spaces and power? What is the role of multilingualism and gender in composing global histories of comparative education? While there are diverse histories in the literature, historiographers can pay more attention to narratives about interflows between 'centre' and 'periphery' in bi- or multi-directional ways. This is what scholars advocate as cross-culturalisation (Takayama 2017; Silova, Millei, and Piattoeva 2017). For such an undertaking, what can comparative education historiographers do? Illustrious thinkers in the field (e.g. Bereday, Hiratsuka, Lauwerys) were polyglots with broad scholarship and educational statesmanship. How can the seed be sown in the future generations of comparative education researchers? Should graduate programmes require a minimum of trilingualism from its students and professors? If so, then which languages would be privileged? What would the consequences of such language policy be?

Overall, what are the implications of asymmetric ignorance in the histories of comparative education? Whose voices are silenced, whose epistemes are invisible? Like the Yin and

Yang principle in Chinese philosophy, all reality is a dialectic of inseparable and contradictory opposites. Mutual recognition and learning, as well as respectful dialogue between opposite intellectual traditions, lead to a holistic and enriching synthesis. Critical insights *from* (not about) the periphery can not only provincialise but also enrich paradigmatic research at the centre. Cowen (2009, 8–9) points to the need for a 'comparative history of comparative education'. He suggested looking into how different iconographies are taken up in the national genealogies of comparative education. For example, is Jullien also recognised as a father of comparative education in say Chinese historical narratives? Some initial attempts have been made to engage the different intellectual and institutional histories of comparative education into some form of cross-cultural dialogue.

Yet the project for future historians is immense. We need new educational statesmen and stateswomen with multilingual skills, historical sense, and a genuine transnational outlook. We need them to venture beyond the 'cave' into new (yet old) spaces and times, seeing alternative forms of 'education' in comparative perspective. We look to them to shed light on comparative education's true origin and identity.

Note

1. CIEclopedia was founded in March 2008 by Teachers College, Columbia University, USA under the leadership of Gita Steiner-Khamsi. The website is currently hosted by the National Institute of Education, Singapore. At the time of writing, the database is in the process of being transferred to its new host, The Education University of Hong Kong under the editorship of Maria Manzon. See http://www.nie.edu.sg/cieclopedia-org/cieclopedia-org-a-to-z-listing (accessed 12 December 2017).

Acknowledgments

I am deeply grateful to Robert Cowen, David Phillips, and Mark Bray for their generous and insightful comments on earlier drafts of this article.

Disclosure statement

No potential conflict of interest was reported by the author.

ORCID

Maria Manzon http://orcid.org/0000-0003-4946-5688

References

Acosta, F., and G. R. Ruiz. 2017. "Revisiting Comparative Education in Latin America: Traditions, Uses and Perspectives." *Comparative Education*, doi:10.1080/03050068.2017.1400760.

Adamson, R. 2015. "Defining a Comparative Identity." In *Changing Times, Changing Territories*, edited by M. Manzon, 39–46. Hong Kong: Comparative Education Research Centre.

Adick, C. 2017. "Bereday and Hilker: Origins of the 'Four Steps of Comparison' Model." *Comparative Education*, doi:10.1080/03050068.2017.1396088.

Albarea, R., ed. 2013. *Conversaciones con un Maestro (Liber Amicorum): Estudio Interdisciplinar de Discípulos y Colegas en Homenaje al Profesor José Luis García Garrido*. Madrid: Ediciones Universitarias, D. L.

Altbach, P. 1991. "Trends in Comparative Education." *Comparative Education* 35 (3): 491–507.

Anderson, B. 2004. *Imagined Communities: Origin and Spread of Nationalism*. London: Verso.

Becher, T., and P. R. Trowler. 2001. *Academic Tribes and Territories: Intellectual Enquiry and the Culture of Disciplines*. 2nd ed. Buckingham;Philadelphia, PA: Society for Research into Higher Education & Open University Press.

Bereday, G. Z. F. 1963. "James Russell's Syllabus of the First Academic Course in Comparative Education." *Comparative Education Review* 7 (2): 189–196.

Bereday, G. Z. F. 1964. *Comparative Method in Education*. New York: Holt, Rinehart and Winston.

Bergh, A.-M., and C. Soudien. 2006. "The Institutionalization of Comparative Education Discourses in South Africa in the 20th Century." *Southern African Review of Education with Education with Production* 12 (2): 35–60.

Bray, M. 2010. "Comparative Education and International Education in the History of *Compare*: Boundaries, Overlaps and Ambiguities." *Compare: A Journal of Comparative and International Education* 40 (6): 711–725.

Bray, M. 2017. "Schooling and its Supplements: Changing Global Patterns and Implications for Comparative Education." *Comparative Education Review* 61 (3): 469–491.

Bray, M., and Q. Gui. 2001. "Comparative Education in Greater China: Contexts, Characteristics, Contrasts and Contributions." *Comparative Education* 37 (4): 451–473.

Bray, M., and M. Manzon. 2014. "The Institutionalization of Comparative Education in Asia and the Pacific: Roles and Contributions of Comparative Education Societies and the WCCES." *Asia Pacific Journal of Education* 34 (2): 228–248.

Broadfoot, P. 2002. "Obituary: Edmund King (1914–2002)." *Comparative Education* 38 (2): 131–132.

Chakrabarty, D. 2000. *Provincializing Europe*. Princeton: Princeton University Press.

Chen, K. H. 2010. *Asia as Method: Toward Deimperialization*. Durham: Duke University Press.

CIES. 2006. *Comparatively Speaking: An Oral History of the First 50 Years of the Comparative and International Education Society (CIES)*. New York: Teachers College, Columbia University.

CIES. 2016. *Comparatively Speaking II: 60 Years of the Comparative and International Education Society (CIES)*. New York: Teachers College, Columbia University.

Cowen, R. 2009. "On History and on the Creation of Comparative Education." In *International Handbook of Comparative Education*, edited by R. Cowen and A. M. Kazamias, 7–10. Dordrecht: Springer.

Cowen, R. 2010. "I Learn Best When I'm on my Feet in Public Failing to Explain Something." Interview by Maria Manzon, 19 March 2009. *CERCular* 12 (1): 4–7. Hong Kong: Comparative Education Research Centre, The University of Hong Kong.

Cowen, R. 2014. "Ways of Knowing, Outcomes, and 'Comparative Education': Be Careful What You Pray For." *Comparative Education* 50 (3): 282–301.

Cowen, R. 2017. "Embodied Comparative Education." *Comparative Education*, doi.org/10.1080/03050068.2017.1409554.

Cowen, R., and A. M. Kazamias, eds. 2009. *International Handbook of Comparative Education*. Dordrecht: Springer Science & Business Media.

Crossley, M., and K. Watson. 2003. *Comparative and International Research in Education. Globalisation, Context and Difference*. London: Routledge Falmer.

Dale, R. 2015. "Conjunctions of Power and Comparative Education." *Compare: A Journal of Comparative and International Education* 45 (3): 341–362.

Epstein, E. H. 2008. "Setting the Normative Boundaries: Crucial Epistemological Benchmarks in Comparative Education." *Comparative Education* 44 (4): 373–386.

Epstein, E. H. 2016a. "Early Leaders: Isaac L. Kandel, William W. Brickman, and C. Arnold Anderson." In *Crafting a Global Field*, edited by E. H. Epstein, 197–208. Dordrecht and Hong Kong: Springer and Comparative Education Research Centre, The University of Hong Kong.

Epstein, E. H., ed. 2016b. *Crafting a Global Field*. Dordrecht and Hong Kong: Springer and Comparative Education Research Centre, The University of Hong Kong.

Epstein, E. H. 2017. "Is Marc-Antoine Jullien de Paris the 'Father' of Comparative Education?" *Compare: A Journal of Comparative and International Education* 47 (3): 317–331.

Erlich, H. 1989. *Students and University in 20th Century Egyptian Politics*. Totowa, NJ: Frank Cass.

Ferrer, F. 2002. *La Educación Comparada Actual*. Barcelona: Ariel.

García Garrido, J. L. 1996. *Fundamentos de Educación Comparada*. Madrid: Editorial Dykinson S.L.

García Garrido, J. L. 2004. "Interview by Maria Manzon, 26 October." Havana, Cuba [in Spanish].

García Garrido, J. L. 2005. "Diez Años de Educación Comparada en España." *Revista Española de Educación Comparada* 11: 15–36.

Gottlieb, E. E. 2000. "Are We Post-modern Yet? Historical and Theoretical Explorations in Comparative Education." In *Routledge International Companion to Education*, edited by M. Ben-Peretz, S. Brown, and B. Moon, 153–176. London: Routledge.

Graham, L., W. Lepenies, and P. Weingart, eds. 1983. *Functions and Uses of Disciplinary Histories*. Dordrecht: D. Reidel.

Gu, M. Y. 2001. "Comparative Education in China: Name and Reality." In *Education in China and Abroad: Perspectives From a Lifetime in Comparative Education*, edited by M. Y. Gu, 236–242. Hong Kong: Comparative Education Research Centre, The University of Hong Kong. Original published in Chinese in *Journal of Foreign Education Studies* 1 (1991).

Gu, M. Y. 2005. "Comparative Education and Me." *Comparative Education Review (Beijing)* 26 (1): 1–4 [in Chinese].

Halls, W.D., ed. 1990. *Comparative Education: Contemporary Issues and Trends*. Paris: UNESCO and London: Jessica Kingsley.

Hayhoe, R. 2004. *Full Circle: A Life with Hong Kong and China*. Hong Kong: Comparative Education Research Centre, The University of Hong Kong.

Hayhoe, R. 2006. *Portraits of Influential Chinese Educators*. Dordrecht and Hong Kong: Springer and Comparative Education Research Centre, The University of Hong Kong.

Holmes, B. 1970. "Nicholas Hans [Obituary]." *Comparative Education Review* 14 (1): 1.

Jullien, M.-A. 1817. *Esquisse et Vues Préliminaires d'un Ouvrage sur l'Éducation Comparée*. Paris: Société Établie à Paris pour l'Amélioration de l'Enseignement Elémentaire. Reprinted 1962. Genève: Bureau International d'Éducation.

Kaloyannaki, P., and A. M. Kazamias. 2009. "The Modernist Beginnings of Comparative Education: The Proto-Scientific and the Reformist-Meliorist Administrative Motif." In *International Handbook of Comparative Education*, edited by R. Cowen and A. M. Kazamias, 11–35. Dordrecht: Springer.

Kazamias, A. M. 2009. "Forgotten Men, Forgotten Themes: The Historical-Philosophical-Cultural and Liberal Humanist Motif in Comparative Education." In *International Handbook of Comparative Education*, edited by R. Cowen and A. M. Kazamias, 37–58. Dordrecht: Springer.

Kelly, G. P., P. Altbach, and R. Arnove. 1982. "Trends in Comparative Education: A Critical Analysis." In *Comparative Education*, edited by P. Altbach, R. Arnove, and G. Kelly, 505–533. New York: Collier Macmillan.

Klein, J. T. 1993. "Blurring, Cracking, and Crossing: Permeation and the Fracturing of Discipline." In *Knowledges: Historical and Critical Studies of Disciplinarity*, edited by E. Messer-Davidson, D. R. Sumway, and D. J. Sylvan, 185–211. Charlottesville: University of Virginia.

Kobayashi, T. 1990. "China, India, Japan and Korea." In *Comparative Education: Contemporary Issues and Trends*, edited by W. D. Halls, 200–226. Paris: UNESCO and London: Jessica Kingsley.

Kodron, C., B von Kopp, U. Lauterbach, U. Schäfer and G. Schmidt, eds. 1997. *Vergleichende Erziehungswissenschaft: Herausforderung, Vermittlung, Praxis. Festchrift für Wolfgang Mitter zum 70 Geburtstag.* Koln: Bohlau.

Larsen, M. A., ed. 2010. *New Thinking in Comparative Education: Honouring Robert Cowen.* Rotterdam: Sense Publishers.

Lázaro, L. M. 2014. "In Memoriam: Julio Ruiz Berrio and Ferrán Ferrer." *Revista Española de Educación Comparada* 23: 9–12.

Leclerq, J-M. 1999. *L'Éducation Comparée: Mondialisation et Spécificités Francophones.* Actes du Congrès International Sur «L'Histoire et l'Avenir de l'Éducation Comparée en Langue Française». Paris: Association Francophone d'Éducation Comparée.

Lee, W. O. 2015. "Pre-history and Foundational Years of CERC." In *Changing Times, Changing Territories*, edited by M. Manzon, 15–26. Hong Kong: Comparative Education Research Centre.

Lenhart, V. 2016. "The First Treatise in Comparative Education Rediscovered." *Research in Comparative and International Education* 11: 222–226.

Lenhart, V. 2017. "Hechtius (1795–1798) – The Beginnings of Historical-Philosophical-Idiographic Research in Comparative Education." *Comparative Education*, doi:10.1080/03050068.2017.1396094.

Macedo, D., P. Gounari, and B. Dendrinos. 2003. *The Hegemony of English.* Boulder: Paradigm.

Manzon, M. 2011. *Comparative Education: The Construction of a Field.* Dordrecht and Hong Kong: Springer and Comparative Education Research Centre, The University of Hong Kong.

Manzon, M., ed. 2015. *Changing Times, Changing Territories: Reflections on CERC and the Field of Comparative Education.* Hong Kong: Comparative Education Research Centre, The University of Hong Kong.

Manzon, M. 2017. "Comparative Education as a Field in Asia: Retrospect and Prospect." *Asia Pacific Journal of Education* 37 (3): 283–298.

Manzon, M., and M. Bray. 2007. "Comparing the Comparers: Patterns, Themes and Interpretations." In *Common Interests, Uncommon Goals: Histories of the World Council of Comparative Education Societies and its Members*, edited by V. Masemann, M. Bray, and M. Manzon, 336–363. Dordrecht and Hong Kong: Springer & Comparative Education Research Centre, The University of Hong Kong.

Marquina, M., and P. Lavia. 2007. "La Formación en Educación Comparada en las Universidades Argentinas: Hacia la Consolidación de un Espacio de Reflexión e Intervención." Paper presented at the second national congress of the Argentinean Comparative Education Society, Buenos Aires.

Martínez, E. 2013. "Educación Comparada en Universidades Sudamericanas: El Caso de Uruguay." In *Comparative Education at Universities World Wide*. 3rd ed, edited by C. Wolhuter, N. Popov, B. Leutwyler, and K. S. Ermenc, 227–236. Sofia: Bureau for Educational Services.

Martínez, M. J., and J. M. Valle. 2005. "10 Años de la REEC. Una Mirada en Perspectiva." *Revista Española de Educación Comparada* 11: 37–93.

Masemann, V., M. Bray, and M. Manzon, eds. 2007. *Common Interests, Uncommon Goals: Histories of the World Council of Comparative Education Societies and Its Members.* Dordrecht and Hong Kong: Springer and Comparative Education Research Centre, The University of Hong Kong.

Masemann, V., S. Majhanovich, N. Truong, and K. Janigan, eds. 2010. *A Tribute to David N. Wilson: Clamouring for a Better World.* Rotterdam: Sense Publishers.

Ninnes, P. 2008. "Fear and Desire in Twentieth Century Comparative Education." *Comparative Education Review* 44 (3): 345–358.

Noah, H. J., and M. A. Eckstein. 1969. *Toward a Science of Comparative Education.* New York: Macmillan.

Nordtveit, B. 2016. "The *Comparative Education Review*." In *Crafting a Global Field*, edited by E. H. Epstein, 140–154. Dordrecht and Hong Kong: Springer and Comparative Education Research Centre, The University of Hong Kong.

Nóvoa, A. 2009. "Empires Overseas and Empires At Home." *Paedagogica Historica* 45 (6): 817–821.

Paulston, R. 1994. "Comparative and International Education: Paradigms and Theories." In *The International Encyclopedia of Education*, edited by T. Husén and T. N. Postlethwaite, 923–933. Oxford: Pergamon Press.

Phillips, D. 2011. "Obituary: Dr. W. D. Halls (1918–2011)." *Comparative Education* 47 (2): 291–293.

Phillips, D., and K. Ochs. 2004. "Researching Policy Borrowing: Some Methodological Challenges in Comparative Education." *British Educational Research Journal* 30 (6): 773–784.

Phillips, D., and M. Schweisfurth. 2014. *Comparative and International Education. An Introduction to Theory, Method and Practice*. 2nd ed. London: Bloomsbury.

Plato. 1963. "Republic: Book VII." In *Plato: Collected Dialogues*, edited by E. Hamilton and H. Cairns (Trans. P. Shorey), 747–752. New York: Random House.

Rapple, B. A. 2017. *Matthew Arnold and English Education: The Poet's Pioneering Advocacy in Middle Class Instruction*. Jefferson, NC: McFarland.

Robertson, L. F., and K. Cushner. 2016. "Early Leaders: Gerald H. Read and George Z. F. Bereday." In *Crafting a Global Field*, edited by E. H. Epstein, 209–217. Dordrecht and Hong Kong: Springer and Comparative Education Research Centre, The University of Hong Kong.

Rosselló, P. 1943. *Marc-Antoine, Jullien de Paris, Père de l'Education Comparée et Précurseur du Bureau International de l'Education*. Geneva: International Bureau of Education.

Schwille, J. 2017. *Internationalizing a School of Education: Integration and Infusion in Practice*. East Lansing, Mich.: Michigan State.

Sen, A. 2004. "Passage to China." *The New York Review of Books*. http://www.nybooks.com/articles/2004/12/02/passage-to-china/. Downloaded 6/4/17.

Silova, I., and W. Brehm. 2014. "For the Love of Knowledge: William W. Brickman and His Comparative Education." *European Education* 42 (2): 11–16.

Silova, I., Z. Millei, and N. Piattoeva. 2017. "Interrupting the Coloniality of Knowledge Production in Comparative Education: Postsocialist and Postcolonial Dialogues after the Cold War." *Comparative Education Review* 61 (S1): S74–S102.

Sobe, N. 2017. "Travelling Researchers, Colonial Difference: Comparative Education in an Age of Exploration." *Compare: A Journal of Comparative and International Education* 47 (3): 332–343.

Takayama, K. 2017. "Towards a New Articulation of Comparative Educations: Cross-culturalising Research Imaginations." *Comparative Education*, doi:10.1080/03050068.2017.1401303.

Takayama, K., A. Sriprakash, and R. Connell. 2017. "Toward a Postcolonial Comparative and International Education." *Comparative Education Review* 61 (S1): S1–S24.

Takekuma, H. 2008. "Comparative Education at Universities in Japan." In *Comparative Education at Universities World Wide*. 2nd ed, edited by C. Wolhuter, N. Popov, M. Manzon, and B. Leutwyler, 229–236. Sofia: Bureau for Educational Services.

Tietze, S., and P. Dick. 2013. "The Victorious English Language: Hegemonic Practices in the Management Academy." *Journal of Management Inquiry* 22 (1): 122–134.

Vilanou, C. Y., and M. Valls. 2001. "En el Centenario del Nacimiento de Juan Tusquets (1901–1998), Propulsor de los Estudios de Pedagogía Comparada en España." *Revista Española de Educación Comparada* 7: 263–294.

Wang, C. 1999. *History of Comparative Education*. Beijing: People's Education Press[in Chinese].

Weidman, J. C., and W. J. Jacob, eds. 2011. *Beyond the Comparative: Advancing Theory and its Application to Practice*. Rotterdam: Sense Publishers.

Welch, A. 1997. "Things Fall Apart: Dis-integration, Universities, and the Decline of Discipline(s). Problematising Comparative Education in an Uncertain Age." In *Vergleichende Erziehungswissenschaft: Herausforderung, Vermittlung, Praxis: Festschrift fur Wolfgang Mitter zum 70. Geburtstag*, edited by C. Kodron, B. von Kopp, U. Lauterbach, U. Schäfer, and G. Schmidt, 182–191. Frankfurt am Main: Bohlau Verlag.

Wilson, D. 1994. "Comparative and International Education: Fraternal or Siamese Twins? A Preliminary Genealogy of Our Twin Fields." *Comparative Education Review* 38 (4): 449–486.

Winther-Jensen, T. 2004. "Nigel Grant–An International Scot." *Comparative Education* 40 (1): 131–136.

Wolhuter, C. C., N. Popov, B. Leutwyler, and K. S. Ermenc, eds. 2013. *Comparative Education at Universities World Wide*. Sofia: Bureau for Educational Services.

Yang, R. 2015. "Viewing CERC Through a Chinese Lens." In *Changing Times, Changing Territories: Reflections on CERC and the Field of Comparative Education*, edited by M. Manzon, 57–62. Hong Kong: Comparative Education Research Centre, The University of Hong Kong.

Index

Note: Page numbers in *italics* refer to figures
Page numbers followed by 'n' refer to notes

Printed in Great Britain
by Amazon